Student Workbook
to accompany

Stress Management for
Wellness

Fourth Edition

Walt Schafer
California State University, Chico

Sharrie A. Herbold
California State University, Chico

Harcourt College Publishers

Fort Worth Philadelphia San Diego New York Orlando Austin San Antonio
Toronto Montreal London Sydney Tokyo

Address for Domestic Orders
Harcourt College Publishers, 6277 Sea Harbor Drive, Orlando, FL 32887-6777
800-782-4479

Address for International Orders
International Customer Service
Harcourt Inc., 6277 Sea Harbor Drive, Orlando, FL 32887-6777
407-345-3800
(fax) 407-345-4060
(e-mail) hbintl@harcourtbrace.com

Address for Editorial Correspondence
Harcourt College Publishers, 301 Commerce Street, Suite 3700, Fort Worth, TX 76102

Web Site Address
http://www.hbcollege.com

Printed in the United States of America

9 0 1 2 3 4 5 6 7 8 202   9 8 7 6 5 4 3 2 1

Harcourt College Publishers

TABLE OF CONTENTS

Application Exercises for CHAPTER 1: The Stress Experience

EXERCISE 1.1
• Rewriting Personal Beliefs About Stress

Consider for a moment the information that you have read in Chapter 1. Write down three beliefs about stress that you had before reading Chapter 1. For example, "all stress has harmful effects on a person's life." Using the information you have learned in Chapter 1, rewrite these beliefs more accurately.

Original Belief #1:

Revised Belief #1:

Original Belief #2:

Revised Belief #2:

Original Belief #3:

Revised Belief #3:

EXERCISE 1.2
• Using The Power Of Interpretation

Think about the last couple of times you have experienced distress. It might have been while in the car, at home, work, or school. Write down the specific stressor you experienced that eventually turned stress into distress. Go back to that stressor now with the knowledge that it is not the demands (stressors) that cause distress (harmful effects), it is your interpretation of that event that causes distress. How could you have interpreted that stressor differently, so distress wasn't the result?

Stressor #1:

New interpretation:

Stressor #2:

New interpretation:

Stressor #3:

New interpretation:

EXERCISE 1.3
• Stress-Related Illnesses And Diseases

Knowing that stress contributes to a number of illnesses and diseases by either aggravating an existing illness, imposing long-term wear and tear on the body and mind, directly causing an illness, or leading to unhealthy coping habits, reflect back to the last time you were sick. Using a separate sheet of paper, write an essay considering the following questions:

- **How could stress have played a part, considering the four linkages mentioned above?**
- **What could you have done differently that might have actually prevented the illness/disease or lessened the severity?**
- **What percentage of your illnesses or diseases in the last few years have been related to stress?**
- **Is your percentage consistent with the research findings that 50 - 80% of all illness episodes are stress-related?**

Harcourt, Inc.

EXERCISE 1.4
• The Costs Of Distress

Distress can have severe costs not only to the individual, but to family members, friends, co-workers, and anyone else that person comes into contact with. Consider the specific costs of distress in your life on both an individual level and a social level. You may also look at the costs of distress to individuals and society in general.

Individual costs of distress:

Social costs of distress:

EXERCISE 1.5
• Utilizing The Power Of Positive Stress

Stress can have very positive effects on one's life. Answer the following questions by considering your current stressors. (You might also consider past stressors that have influenced your life positively.)

1. Which stressors are having (or could have) a positive effect on your life?

2. Explain why they have had (or could have) a positive effect on your life.

Harcourt, Inc.

EXERCISE 1.6
• The Social Context Of Stress

Find three current articles from either the Internet, a newspaper, or a periodical that illustrate how individual stress levels are influenced by the larger social structure, either positively or negatively.

Article #1 Summary:

Influence:

Article #2 Summary:

Influence:

Article #3 Summary:

Influence:

Harcourt, Inc.

EXERCISE 1.7
• Quality-of-Life Assessment

Answer the following self-assessment questions. After you have completed the assessment, use Exercise 1.8 to reflect upon your responses.

1. Circle the number below that best describes how much *in control of your own life* you feel these days.

   1   2   3   4   5   6   7   8   9   10

   Not at all   **Moderately**   **Completely**
   in control   **in control**   **in control**

2. Circle the number below that best describes your *emotional tension* these days.

   1   2   3   4   5   6   7   8   9   10

   No emotional   **Moderate**   **A great deal**
   tension at all   **emotional**   **of emotional**
                                    tension   **tension**

3. Circle the number below that best describes your feeling of *depression* these days.

   1   2   3   4   5   6   7   8   9   10

   No depression   **Moderate**   **A great deal**
   at all   **depression**   **of depression**

4. Circle the number below that best describes how *satisfied* you are with *life as a whole* these days.

   1   2   3   4   5   6   7   8   9   10

   Not at all   **Moderately**   **Completely**
   satisfied   **satisfied**   **satisfied**

5. Circle the number below that best describes how *satisfied* you are with your *health* these days.

   1   2   3   4   5   6   7   8   9   10

   Not at all   **Moderately**   **Completely**
   satisfied   **satisfied**   **satisfied**

6. Circle the number below that best describes how *satisfied* you are with your *job* these days.

   1   2   3   4   5   6   7   8   9   10

   Not at all   **Moderately**   **Completely**
   satisfied   **satisfied**   **satisfied**

7. Circle the number below that best describes how *satisfied* you are with your *home life* these days.

   1   2   3   4   5   6   7   8   9   10

   Not at all   **Moderately**   **Completely**
   satisfied   **satisfied**   **satisfied**

8. Circle the number below that best describes how *optimistic* you are about your *health* during the next five years.

   1   2   3   4   5   6   7   8   9   10

   Not at all   **Moderately**   **Completely**
   optimistic   **optimistic**   **optimistic**

Harcourt, Inc.

9. Circle the number below that best describes how *optimistic* you are about your *life as a whole* during the next five years.

1	2	3	4	5	6	7	8	9	10

Not at all optimistic   **Moderately optimistic**   **Completely optimistic**

10. Circle the number below that best describes how *happy* you are these days, all things considered.

1	2	3	4	5	6	7	8	9	10

Not at all happy   **Moderately happy**   **Completely happy**

11. Circle the number below that best describes how much *fun and playfulness* you are having these days.

1	2	3	4	5	6	7	8	9	10

None at all   **Moderate amount**   **A great deal**

12. Circle the number below that best describes your *self-esteem* or *self-liking* these days.

1	2	3	4	5	6	7	8	9	10

Very low self-esteem   **Moderate self-esteem**   **Very high self-esteem**

13. Circle the number below that best describes your *sense of vitality* or *energy level* these days.

1	2	3	4	5	6	7	8	9	10

Very low energy level   **Moderate energy level**   **Very high energy level**

EXERCISE 1.8
• Learning From Your Quality-of-Life Assessment

Answer the following questions to learn more about your quality of life.

1. How satisfied are you with the picture you see of yourself through these scores? Be specific.

2. Which scores would you especially like to improve? Why?

3. What would it take within yourself, in your life circumstances, or both, to improve your scores?

CHAPTER 1 SELF-TEST

Instructions: Circle true or false. Answers can be found in the appendix.

1. Demands do not cause harmful effects, the harmful effects result from the person's interpretation of the demands.
   True   **False**

2. Approximately one-third of all illness and diseases are stress-related.
   True   **False**

3. The common cold and cancer are examples of how stress directly causes an illness or disease.
   True   **False**

4. Headaches, depression, psoriasis, heart attacks, and colitis are all stress-related diseases.
   True   **False**

5. Distress has only harmful effects.
   True   **False**

6. The costs of distress affect only the individual who is experiencing the distress.
   True   **False**

7. Personal growth comes through pushing your limits beyond what is immediately comfortable.
   True   **False**

8. A person's social environment plays a small role in determining the amount of stress experienced.
   True   **False**

9. Egoistic altruism explains the effect ego has on stress levels.
   True   **False**

10. Constructive maladjustment refers to people who need to adjust the way they handle stress.
    True   **False**

Application Exercises for CHAPTER 2:
Passing the Test of College Stress

EXERCISE 2.1

• Clustering Of Life Changes

Think of a previous time in your life when you experienced a number of life changes in a short period of time. Write a brief essay considering the following questions:

- **Could you have decreased the number of changes? Maybe waited to make a change or two?**
- **How did you cope with the life changes you were experiencing?**
- **As a result of the life changes, did you experience distress (emotionally, cognitively, physically, or socially)?**
- **What could you have done differently?**

Now consider your future. Write a brief essay considering the following questions:
- **Are you anticipating a clustering of life changes in the future? Maybe you are graduating soon, getting married, starting a new job, and moving.**
- **How might you decrease the number of changes experienced in a short period of time?**
- **If the changes cannot be decreased, how do you plan to minimize distress that often accompanies a clustering of life changes?**

EXERCISE 2.2
• Love, Sex, And Stress

Consider some of the following concerns involving love, sex, and stress listed in the box below.

Sexual Harassment	Commitment
Sexual Assault (Rape, Date Rape, Acquaintance Rape)	Sexual Intercourse
Unwanted Pregnancy	Intimacy
Sexually Transmitted Diseases	Relationships
Sexual Orientation	Peer Pressure

1. Which of these concerns affect you currently?

2. How are you presently dealing with those concerns?

3. How might you cope with those concerns to minimize the amount of distress you experience?

4. How might you prevent distress in specific situations that involve love, sex, and stress?

EXERCISE 2.3
• Role Difficulties

A role is a cluster of expectations associated with a given social position. Most people have a handful of roles they fulfill at a given time in their life. For example, one person may have the role of a spouse, parent, student, employee, daughter, friend, and sister. Because we are fulfilling a number of roles at a given time, it is not surprising that distress can often result from these roles. Consider the questions below concerning the role difficulties present in your life.

1. Which role difficulties (role conflict, role overload, role strain, or role ambiguity) are you currently experiencing?

2. What change(s), if any, could you make that could decrease or eliminate the presence of role difficulty in your life?

3. What distress symptoms do you think result from these role difficulties?

4. If these role difficulties are unavoidable, how might you minimize their harmful effects on your personal stress level?

Harcourt, Inc.

EXERCISE 2.4
• Alcohol And Stress

Considering alcohol is used more frequently than any other drug (other than caffeine and nicotine), evaluate your personal experience with alcohol by writing a brief essay. Consider the following questions:

- **How often do you drink?**
- **What are the reasons you drink?**
- **Is there a relationship between your drinking patterns and stress?**
- **Why is alcohol use considered a maladaptive (negative) coping response to stress?**
- **What can be done to decrease the incidence in which alcohol is used as a coping method in our society, especially among college students?**

EXERCISE 2.5
• Evaluating Life Scripts

Consider some of your life scripts that have emerged during childhood and adolescence out of early messages from parents and other adults. Can you think of some positive life scripts that contribute to your overall well-being? Can you think of some negative life scripts that you'd like to change because of their negative effect on your overall well-being? Remember life scripts manifest a strong hold on our behavior because humans naturally have the drive to do what is familiar, so you will want to solidify the steps in making the changes. Take a few moments to write out a plan for changing a specific life script.

Current life scripts that I would like to keep.....

Current life scripts that I would like to change.....

A current life script that I would most like to change is.......

How will I recognize this specific life script?

When I recognize the life script, I will.....

The behavior or response I will substitute for the old life script is......

Harcourt, Inc.

EXERCISE 2.6
• Examining Episodes Of College Stress

The college experience can provide a person with a strong foundation for a successful future, but it doesn't usually happen without obstacles and challenges. The college years are full of stressors, both positive and negative. Learning to cope positively with the negative stressors will increase your chances of "Passing the Test of College Stress." Answer the following questions to assess the current distressors you are experiencing that are associated with your "college experience."

1. List the three to five most distressing episodes during your past year or two in school.

2. For each episode, what was (were) the precipitating distressor(s)?

3. For each episode, what coping steps or processes did you use? With what outcomes?

4. Looking back, what coping methods, if any, might you have used that would have been more effective?

Harcourt, Inc.

EXERCISE 2.7
• Building Confidence

The figure below presents a model for understanding how confidence grows. Using this figure, answer the following questions to assess your confidence qualities.

BUILDING CONFIDENCE

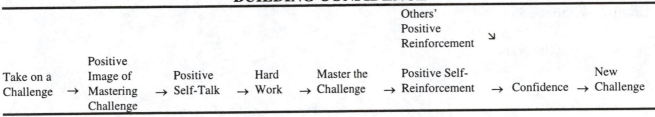

1. **What are your strengths and weaknesses in the confidence-building process shown above?**

2. **Which components in the confidence-building process will you strengthen during coming weeks?**

3. **What specific steps will you take to make this happen?**

4. **How might this model of confidence building be applied by parents to build confidence in their children? Be specific.**

Harcourt, Inc.

EXERCISE 2.8
• Passing The Test Of College Stress

If you were writing a book entitled "Passing the Test of College Stress," what would be the titles of your chapters? What advice could you give to college students that would help them succeed during the college years?

Chapter 1 Title:

Summary of Chapter:

Chapter 2 Title:

Summary of Chapter:

Chapter 3 Title:

Summary of Chapter:

Chapter 4 Title:

Summary of Chapter:

Chapter 5 Title:

Summary of Chapter:

Chapter 6 Title:

Summary of Chapter:

Chapter 7 Title:

Summary of Chapter:

Harcourt, Inc.

CHAPTER 2 SELF-TEST

Instructions: Circle true or false. Answers can be found in the appendix.

1. Research has shown a positive correlation between the clustering of life changes and the risk of illness and other difficulties.
   True   **False**

2. It appears that acute stressors wear an individual down more mentally and physically when compared to daily hassles.
   True   **False**

3. People with an external locus of control are less vulnerable to distress because they believe their lifestyle choices directly influence their life.
   True   **False**

4. A key point about daily hassles is that the interpretation of these events determines how stressful or irritating they become.
   True   **False**

5. Using mental rehearsal is a way of preventing test anxiety that arises from negative mental images.
   True   **False**

6. Inadequate preparation leads to poor test performance, but it doesn't lead to test anxiety.
   True   **False**

7. Jack Adams would rather go to the movies rather than work on his homework assignment. This illustrates role ambiguity.
   True   **False**

8. Sandra Johnson is torn between the expectations of her instructors and her boss. This illustrates role overload.
   True   **False**

9. Alcohol is used more frequently than any other drug (excluding caffeine and nicotine).
   True   **False**

10. Life scripts most often contribute to one's wellness.
    True   **False**

Application Exercises for CHAPTER 3: Wellness

EXERCISE 3.1
• RUWell Assessment

RUWell is a wellness assessment based on the seven dynamic dimensions of wellness (Physical, Social, Emotional, Intellectual, Environmental, Spiritual, and Time). Researchers refer to the dimensions as dynamic because they are constantly changing. Each dimension is affected by the other. As you read through the RUWell assessment, take note of how one dimension of wellness may affect other areas of wellness. The purpose of the RUWell assessment is to provide you with an increased awareness about your individual wellness. With this increased awareness you can identify which dimensions of wellness you are currently satisfied with and which dimensions could use some improvement. Check the answer that best fits your response to each of the statements listed below.

PHYSICAL DIMENSION

Almost Always	Sometimes	Almost Never	
			I am physically active at least four times per week for 30 minutes.
			I drink at least 64 ounces of water every day.
			I eat at least five servings of fruits and vegetables every day.
			I eat breakfast every morning.
			I get approximately 8 hours of sleep every night.
			I choose to avoid the use of tobacco products and my exposure to tobacco smoke.
			I examine my breasts or testes on a monthly basis.
			I maintain normal blood pressure. (If you do not know your blood pressure, answer "almost never".)
			I wear my seat belt regularly.
			I am satisfied with my energy levels.

SOCIAL DIMENSION

Almost Always	Sometimes	Almost Never	
			I am appropriately concerned about unacceptable social conditions.
			I stay current on the state of world affairs.
			I exercise my right to vote.
			I enjoy helping others (including strangers, family, and friends).
			I enjoy my work.
			I am comfortable meeting new people in a variety of settings.
			I participate in a wide variety of groups, including educational, recreational, religious, and occupational groups.
			I contribute time and/or money to at least one organization that strives to better my community.
			I take time to spend "quality" time with my family and friends.
			I possess good communication skills (both giving and receiving).

Harcourt, Inc.

EMOTIONAL DIMENSION

Almost Always	Sometimes	Almost Never	
			I am able to express my anger positively.
			I believe there are no such things as mistakes, only different degrees of success.
			My intimate relationships are satisfying.
			Humor is a part of my daily life.
			I see change as a positive experience and accept its presence with a sense of confidence.
			I can manage the stress in my life.
			I resolve conflict in a respectful manner.
			I take time out for myself without feeling guilty.
			I allow myself to experience a variety of emotions and find positive ways to express them.
			I have a strong sense of confidence and self-esteem.

INTELLECTUAL WELLNESS

Almost Always	Sometimes	Almost Never	
			I am able to concentrate easily.
			I enjoy learning.
			I make decisions with a minimum amount of stress and worry.
			I enjoy learning about different topics from a variety of mediums (e.g., the Internet, books, newspapers, and magazines).
			I am aware of the influence my social environment has on my thinking.
			I use my sense of creativity to solve problems.
			I am skeptical and demonstrate critical thinking.
			I am open minded.
			I am able to express my opinions and feelings to others easily.
			I learn from my life experiences.

ENVIRONMENTAL DIMENSION

Almost Always	Sometimes	Almost Never	
			I recycle various materials.
			I conserve energy and materials at home, school, and work.
			I take my own bags when shopping.
			I am concerned about the presence of pesticides when buying food products.
			I turn the water off when I'm brushing my teeth, washing my car, shaving, etc.
			I use alternative transportation (e.g., walk, bike, rollerblade, and skateboard) or carpool whenever possible.
			I purchase recyclable or biodegradable products.
			I am interested in learning more about how I can preserve natural resources.
			I consciously reduce the amount of waste I produce.
			I am concerned about the global environment and its effects on the quality of life.

Harcourt, Inc.

SPIRITUAL DIMENSION

Almost Always	Sometimes	Almost Never	
			Making time for prayer or other spiritual behavior is part of my regular routine.
			My values and morals affect my daily behavior and choices.
			My life has a positive direction and meaning.
			I help others who are less fortunate than I.
			I seek comfort and support from my faith when needed.
			I see myself as a part of a "bigger" picture.
			I am able to discuss my own death with family and friends.
			I see the future as an opportunity for personal growth.
			I am satisfied with the direction of my spirituality.
			My daily behavior and life long choices are largely influenced by internal factors rather than external factors.

TIME DIMENSION

Almost Always	Sometimes	Almost Never	
			I am satisfied with the balance between my work time and leisure time.
			I maintain a comfortable pace of life.
			I am satisfied with my ability to manage and control my workload.
			I do not feel unreasonably hurried in my daily routine.
			I don't have problems getting started on large tasks or projects.
			I make time in my daily routine for relaxation and play.
			I maintain control over my time.
			I do not procrastinate.
			I regularly prioritize and schedule my daily tasks.
			I practice the concept of simplicity whenever possible to minimize overload in my life.

Congratulations! You have completed the RUWell assessment. Please take a moment to reflect upon your scores in each category. In which dimensions did you mostly answer "Almost Always?" These dimensions represent positive areas of your individual wellness. In which dimensions did you mostly answer "Almost Never?" You may want to strive to enhance your level of wellness by making some positive changes in these dimensions. Remember one dimension is not more important than another. For a high level of wellness to occur, all dimensions must positively work together. Perhaps you could begin by improving your weakest dimension and set a realistic goal for improvement by using Exercise 3.2. Good luck in reaching a higher level of wellness. Be Well!

Harcourt, Inc.

EXERCISE 3.2
• Making A Change For The "Well" Of It!

After completing the RUWell assessment you should be more aware of the wellness habits that you could change or strengthen. Take a few minutes to decide on a specific area that you would like to change. Use the behavior change form below to assist you with the change you would like to make. Having a specific plan for change ensures success!

MY CONTRACT FOR MAKING A CHANGE

The current date is: _____

The specific change I would like to make is: _____
_____

Factors that will motivate me to make this change include: _____
_____
_____
_____
_____

Specific steps I will take to make these changes include: _____
_____
_____
_____

My start date for making these changes is: _____

The way in which I will keep track of my progress includes: _____
_____
_____

If I need help, I will: _____
_____

My target date for reaching this goal is: _____

A reward for achieving this goal is: _____
_____

My signature: _____ **My supporter's signature:** _____

Harcourt, Inc.

EXERCISE 3.3
• Evaluating Cultures Of Wellness Or Worseness

A culture of wellness consists of those features of a group or organization that encourage, reward, and support wellness choices. A culture of worseness is made up of those features of the social environment that discourage healthy choices and encourage, reward, and support unhealthy, unwholesome choices. Using the questions below, reflect upon your own cultures of wellness and worseness.

1. Which organizations or groups that you are involved with encourage, reward, and support wellness choices? How can you increase the number of cultures of wellness you have in your life?

2. Which organizations or groups that you are involved with discourage healthy choices and encourage, reward, and support unwholesome choices? How can you decrease the number of cultures of worseness you have in your life?

3. Give specific examples of how you personally contribute to a culture of worseness and/or a culture of wellness.

Harcourt, Inc.

EXERCISE 3.4
• Assessing Your Energy Type

Possessing maximum energy for daily living is considered a key element of wellness. One way to evaluate your current energy level is to use the energy types as described by Davis (1980). Answer the questions below to evaluate your current energy type.

1. Which energy type (stroller, jogger, sprinter, or long-distance athlete) best describes you?

2. Are you currently satisfied with your energy type? Give specific examples that support your answer.

3. What factors have influenced your energy type? Hereditary factors? Environmental factors? Personal choices?

4. What changes will you make, if needed, to alter the current intensity or endurance of your energy?

Harcourt, Inc.

EXERCISE 3.5
• Assessing Your Energy Qualities

Answer the following self-assessment questions. After you are finished, use the questions below the assessment to reflect upon your answers.

1. Circle the number below that best describes how *natural* or *nervous* your energy tends to be these days.

1	2	3	4	5	6	7	8	9	10

**Very
nervous**   **A mixture
of both**   **Very
natural**

2. Circle the number below that best describes how *satisfying* or *unsatisfying* your energy is these days.

1	2	3	4	5	6	7	8	9	10

**Very
unsatisfying**   **A mix
of both**   **Very
satisfying**

3. Circle the number below that best describes how *helpful* or *harmful* your energy is these days.

1	2	3	4	5	6	7	8	9	10

**Very
harmful**   **A mix
of both**   **Very
helpful**

4. Circle the number below that best describes how *directed* or *wasted* your energy is these days.

1	2	3	4	5	6	7	8	9	10

**Very
wasted**   **A mix
of both**   **Very
directed**

• What have you learned about your quality of energy after completing this self-appraisal?

• What specific changes will you make to improve your energy quality, if needed?

EXERCISE 3.6
• Unblocking Energy

Blocked energy interferes with the ability to reach our full potential. Several factors, such as negative self-talk, negative personality traits, fear, unexpressed emotions, a lack of self confidence, unhealthy lifestyle choices, and unhealthy relationships, can contribute to blocked energy.

1. **List at least five specific ways in which you block your energy.**

2. **What specific steps will you take to prevent the blocking of energy?**

3. **What specific steps will you take to unblock your energy?**

EXERCISE 3.7
• Maximizing Daily Energy For Optimal Living

The majority of people in our society often wish they had more energy for daily living. Energy levels can be increased by implementing positive lifestyle habits. Consider the following statements:

To develop a more even daily energy pattern, I will:

In order to increase my energy level during the next three months, I will:

CHAPTER 3 SELF-TEST

Instructions: Circle true or false. Answers can be found in the appendix.

1. Wellness is the continuous process of achieving full human potential.
    True   **False**

2. Being a critical thinker and open to new ideas are characteristics of the emotional dimension of wellness.
    True   **False**

3. Resiliency, resolving conflict in a respectful manner, and managing stress are all characteristics of the spiritual dimension of wellness.
    True   **False**

4. The likelihood of a person developing a wellness lifestyle is influenced only by personal choice.
    True   **False**

5. The American Heart Association is an example of a culture of wellness.
    True   **False**

6. Research suggests that high levels of perceived personal energy doesn't affect a person's distress level.
    True   **False**

7. The relaxation response helps restore energy and increases a person's energy level.
    True   **False**

8. A person who has short bursts of high energy would best be described as a jogger.
    True   **False**

9. The two key dimensions of energy are duration and endurance.
    True   **False**

10. Negative self-talk, low self-esteem, and unexpressed feelings can block a person's energy.
    True   **False**

Application Exercises for CHAPTER 4:
The Dynamics of Stress and Relaxation

EXERCISE 4.1
• Mind-Body-Behavior And Wellness

Considering the strong link between mind-body-behavior, write a brief essay discussing specific ways in which a person can increase their individual wellness by utilizing these linkages.

EXERCISE 4.2
• Mind-Body-Behavior And Social Implications

Write a brief essay explaining some benefits that our society would receive if more emphasis was placed on the mind-body-behavior linkages. Consider health care costs, quality of life, crime rates, and other sociological factors.

EXERCISE 4.3
• Adaptation To Stress

You read in Chapter 4 that adaptation to stress has two meanings. First, you raise your threshold of distress as your mind and body become accustomed to a given level of arousal or exertion. This is illustrated by the training effect during athletic training. As your body experiences progressively more cardiovascular or muscular demands, your body successfully adapts to these demands. The same holds true in your life. As you become accustomed to the demands of a new job, a challenging relationship at work, or a level of academic challenge, your mind adapts to successfully meet these demands. Second, you learn to adapt to distress. Although the pain or discomfort remains, you learn to live with it, as in a period of loss, extreme financial hardship, or a period of intense and temporary overload. With this in mind, answer the questions below.

1. **Describe an example of either type of adaptation mentioned above that you have experienced in the past.**

2. **Describe the circumstances that were involved.**

3. **What were your mental, physical, and behavioral symptoms of distress as you entered the experience?**

4. **Did the symptoms diminish as you adapted? Or did you simply become accustomed to the distress? Explain.**

Harcourt, Inc.

EXERCISE 4.4
• Monitor Your Heart Rate

This exercise is intended to increase your awareness of the physiological arousal you experience during a typical day. Using the table below, monitor and record your heart rate (use beats per minute, bpm, for your measurement) for an entire day. Your pulse rate can be measured at the carotid artery (one on either side of the Adam's apple at the front of your neck) or at the radial artery (on the inside of your wrist, just above the base of the thumb). Once you have found a regular pulse, look at the second hand of a watch. Count the number of beats you feel in a 10-second period and multiply this number by 6. This number will be your heart rate. Begin monitoring and recording your heart rate when you first wake up, before you even get out of bed, and continue to monitor and record your heart rate once per hour for the entire day. Be sure to indicate the specific activity you are engaged in when you monitor your heart rate. Also monitor and record your heart rate during and immediately after any high-stress experiences you may have during the day. Be sure to practice at least one relaxation exercise during the day and make a note of your heart rate before and after the exercise.

Activity	Time	Heart Rate
Resting Heart Rate (check your heart rate before getting out of bed)		

Harcourt, Inc.

EXERCISE 4.5
• Exhaustion, Illness, And Disease

The last stage in Selye's General Adaptation Syndrome (GAS), exhaustion, explains how stress is related to disease and illness. Consider the last time you got sick or acquired a disease. Write a brief essay describing the obstacles that prevented you from achieving homeostasis, thereby causing the illness or disease.

EXERCISE 4.6
• Stress And Surgical Complications

One example of how the stress response can affect the mind and body is the risk of surgical complications. Some physicians are beginning to recognize that stress not only affects a surgical patient's ability to recover quickly and completely, but can also increase the number of surgical complications. Use the information in Chapter 4 on stress and surgical complications to answer the questions below.

1. **What are some practical implications of the stress and surgical complications study (discussed in Chapter 4) for medical practice?**

2. **What are some implications of this study for you personally?**

Harcourt, Inc.

CHAPTER 4 SELF-TEST

Instructions: Circle true or false. Answers can be found in the appendix.

1. Lipragus is a good example of the strong linkages between the mind, body, and behavior.
    True   **False**

2. The central nervous system is divided into two main parts: the sympathetic nervous system and the parasympathetic nervous system.
    True   **False**

3. The pituitary gland is considered the key link in the stress response because it regulates the sympathetic nervous system, the parasympathetic nervous system, and the endocrine system.
    True   **False**

4. The two main hormones (catecholamines) responsible for providing energy during the stress response are adrenaline and epinephrine.
    True   **False**

5. The body is prepared for direct decisive physical action through the sympathetic nervous system and the endocrine system.
    True   **False**

6. The adrenal cortex secretes the catecholamines into the bloodstream when it is stimulated by the sympathetic nervous system.
    True   **False**

7. When the body is ready for direct, decisive, physical action and we choose not to act (physical inaction), bound energy, tension, and distress are likely to occur.
    True   **False**

8. Research shows that stress can reduce one's immunocompetence.
    True   **False**

9. According to the General Adaptation Syndrome (GAS), your body mobilizes additional resources to re-establish homeostasis during the alarm stage.
    True   **False**

10. Some research suggests deeper rest may occur during deliberately induced deep relaxation than during sleep.
    True   **False**

Application Exercises for CHAPTER 5: How the Stress Experience Varies

EXERCISE 5.1

• Sensory Deprivation

A number of laboratory experiments on sensory deprivation, the extreme of underload, demonstrate that most people soon begin to experience disorientation, anxiety, depression, or other discomforts when deprived of light, touch, sound, and smell. Using the space below, describe other ways in which sensory deprivation can negatively affect one's wellness.

EXERCISE 5.2
• Residual Stress

Experts recommend two of the best ways to cope with residual stress are through journal writing and talking to others. Think of a residual stressor you are dealing with, then use the following space below to describe the specific situation or event. Be sure to include feelings, thoughts, and behavior associated with the event. If you aren't experiencing residual stress, use the space below to explain why journal writing or talking to others has been proven effective in dealing with residual stressors.

Harcourt, Inc.

EXERCISE 5.3
• Anticipatory Stress

Consider a specific situation or event in which you sometimes experience anticipatory stress, either positive or negative. Describe the specific stressor, your self-talk (your thoughts, interpretation, or internal dialogue) about the situation or event, and the result or consequence of your anticipatory stress.

1. A situation or event in which I experience anticipatory stress is:

2. Examples of my self-talk include:

3. Consequences of my anticipatory stress are:

4. I might change my self-talk to change the consequences next time I experience this specific situation by:

Harcourt, Inc.

EXERCISE 5.4
• Assessing Your Zone Of Positive Stress

Each person possesses his or her own zone of positive stress--the tolerance range of stress in which the person is healthy, productive, and satisfied. Complete the following exercise to assess your individual zone of positive stress.

1. **Using the numerical scale ranging from 0 to 100, indicate your upper and lower limits.**

POSITIVE STRESS ZONE

Very High Stress

100 _____

90 _____

80 _____

70 _____

60 _____

50 _____

40 _____

30 _____

20 _____

10 _____

Very Low Stress

0 _____

2. **What are some of your warning signs that indicate you've reached either the upper or lower limits of your zone of positive stress?**

3. **Are you currently satisfied with the upper and lower limits of your zone of positive stress? Consider how well your zone of positive stress matches up with the demands of your environment.**

4. **How might you expand your current zone of positive stress to improve your overall wellness?**

Harcourt, Inc.

EXERCISE 5.5
• People Who Illustrate Each Of The Six Ways Of Relating To Stress

In the spaces below, briefly describe someone you know who illustrates each of the six ways of relating to stress. You may also include media figures. If you are describing someone you know, you may or may not want to write an actual name. In either event, write down the personal habits or characteristics that lead you to see the person this way.

Stress-seeker:

Stress-avoider:

Distress-seeker:

Distress-avoider:

Distress-provoker:

Distress-reducer:

CHAPTER 5 SELF-TEST

Instructions: Circle true or false. Answers can be found in the appendix.

1. According to the experience continuum, distress can arise from either over- or under-stimulation.
    True   **False**

2. Qualitative overload results from too much to do in the time available.
    True   **False**

3. Anticipatory stress always results in distress.
    True   **False**

4. Researchers have found that people who experience residual stress can minimize distress by writing about the traumatic experiences.
    True   **False**

5. The zone of positive stress is the tolerance range within which a person is healthy, productive, and satisfied.
    True   **False**

6. Each person possesses three zones of stress: a zone of positive stress, a zone of negative stress, and a zone of neutral stress.
    True   **False**

7. When a person's baseline stress level is too high, hair-trigger stress reaction, too high peak stress, and stress build-up are more likely to occur.
    True   **False**

8. Distress-seekers thrive on challenge, risk, and sensation.
    True   **False**

9. A person who seeks to do everything possible to promote the well-being of others and to minimize distress for them is called a stress-reducer.
    True   **False**

10. A powerful internal drive of habit is known as repetition compulsion.
    True   **False**

Application Exercises for CHAPTER 6: Distress Symptoms

EXERCISE 6.1
• Using Anxiety To Enhance Performance

Anxiety can be a very useful tool for enhancing performance. A person wants to utilize the natural anxiety that occurs before an event to maximize performance. Complete the statements below to assist you in learning how you might benefit from using anxiety for optimal performance in all areas of your life.

The situations in which I most often experience anxiety include.....

My self-talk statements before I experience the specific situation include....

My self-talk statements during the specific situation include....

Rewrite the self-talk statements given above in a more positive manner. Using the new self-talk statements before and during the specific situations listed above may prevent anxiety from turning into distress.

Harcourt, Inc.

EXERCISE 6.2
• Depression Assessment

Depression is known as the "common cold" of emotional disorders because it is the most common emotional disorder in the U.S. Depression, as well as all emotional disorders, affect not only emotional well-being, but behavioral, physical, and cognitive well-being as well. The "bad news" concerning depression is that it is so common and often people don't seek help because of the social stigma attached to "mental illnesses." People should see emotional strains, such as depression, for what they really are, acute stress, too much stress for too long, or a harmful reaction to stress, rather than mental illness. The "good news" concerning depression is that the majority of depressed people can be successfully treated with medication, therapy, lifestyle modifications or a combination of all three. Use the assessment below to learn more about which symptoms of depression you've been experiencing during the last few months.

DURING THE LAST FEW MONTHS.....	FREQUENTLY	SOMETIMES	NEVER
I haven't had enough energy to meet my daily demands.			
I have been withdrawn from interactions with others in my life.			
I have felt a sense of helplessness in regards to my life.			
I haven't been able to find joy in my usual "pleasurable" activities.			
I have experienced feelings of sadness.			
I have been unusually irritable.			
I have experienced an extreme change in my sleeping habits.			
I have experienced an extreme change in my eating habits.			
It is difficult to get up in the morning and/or leave the house.			

Complete the following questions to learn more about how depression is affecting your wellness. Use a separate piece of paper, if more space is needed.

1. After completing the assessment above, explain how depression is currently affecting your wellness.

2. If depression is currently affecting your wellness, what lifestyle modifications can you implement that will help you regain normal function? If you feel you would benefit from medication, therapy or both, how will you go about getting help? If depression isn't currently affecting your wellness, explain what factors in your life reduce the incidence of depression.

Harcourt, Inc.

EXERCISE 6.3
• Monitoring Your Anger

Consistent research findings have shown that anger is a very toxic personality trait. For example, some researchers have found that angry people die prematurely when compared to their non-angry peers. Even though anger can be positive, if it leads to constructive problem-solving, most often anger has a negative effect on a person's wellness. Use the questions below to become more aware of your anger patterns and how you deal with the anger in your life.

1. **Describe at least two specific situations in which you were easily angered in the last month.**

   Situation #1:

   Situation #2:

2. **Exactly what did you feel emotionally and physically at the moment of anger? One hour later? Four hours later?**

	At the moment	**One hour later**	**Four hours later**
Situation #1:			
Situation #2:			

3. **How did you handle the anger? Was this a constructive or destructive response to your anger?**

   Situation #1:

   Situation #2:

4. **Looking back, what might you have done differently in handling the anger to minimize distress for yourself and others?**

   Situation #1:

   Situation #2:

Harcourt, Inc.

EXERCISE 6.4
• The F.U.D Factor vs. The N.I.C.E Factor

Fear is part of the F.U.D factor (Fear, Uncertainty, and Doubt). Some researchers suggest these three factors are the root cause of distress for most people because fear, uncertainty, and doubt contribute to a perceived lack of control. Often these three factors are the direct result of negative self-talk. Therefore, to minimize the amount of distress caused by fear, a person needs to change their self-talk. Instead of using the F.U.D factors, use the N.I.C.E factors. N.I.C.E factors include (New, Interesting, Challenging, and Exciting) (Hope Newsletter, Feb. 1996). Write a brief essay considering the following questions:

• **What fears do you currently have?**

• **How might you change your current self-talk to minimize the fear you currently experience? Consider using self-talk statements that utilize the N.I.C.E factors.**

Harcourt, Inc.

EXERCISE 6.5
• How Do You React To Frustration?

Frustration is a part of life. We often feel frustrated because something or someone is keeping us from what we want to have, experience, or do. The key to minimizing distress from frustration is to look at how you react to it. Write a brief essay below considering the following questions:

- **Think of the last few times you experienced frustration. How did you react--hyperreactive, nonreactive, or simply reactive?**
- **What was the outcome of the situation?**
- **How might you simply react the next time you experience frustration so the outcome can be positive?**

EXERCISE 6.6
• Negative And Positive Implications Of Guilt

Guilt is a common type of emotional distress. People feel guilty when they regret something they have done or said or something that they will do or say. Feelings of guilt can have both positive and negative implications. The positive implications of guilt are apparent when those feelings motivate us to make amends or to avoid repeating the behavior that elicited the guilty feelings. The negative implications of guilt are apparent when a person can't let go of the guilt and those feelings interfere with a person's wellness. Answer the following questions below to better understand how you use guilt in your life.

1. **In your own words, what is guilt?**

2. **In the past, when has feeling guilty had positive implications on your life?**

3. **In what specific circumstances do you most often experience guilt? Exactly how do you feel? What other emotions accompany guilt?**

4. **How do you respond to your feelings of guilt? What are the results for you and others in your life?**

Harcourt, Inc.

EXERCISE 6.7
• Monitoring Your Emotional Distress Symptoms

Learning to recognize your emotional distress symptoms can help you understand that these symptoms often serve as warning signs that something is wrong and needs to be changed. Emotional distress symptoms may reflect positive, temporary arousal associated with an intense but positively challenging situation or they may reflect more troublesome, ongoing distress. Answer the following questions to become more aware of the emotional distress symptoms in your life.

1. **During the past two weeks, which common emotional distress symptoms have you experienced?**

2. **Which of these emotional distress symptoms do you experience most frequently and repeatedly over the long run?**

3. **What stressors tend to precipitate these symptoms?**

Harcourt, Inc.

EXERCISE 6.8
• Monitoring Your Cognitive Distress Symptoms

Cognitive distress symptoms can also serve as warning signs that something is wrong and needs to be changed. Often cognitive distress symptoms reflect the internal pressures of experiencing overload in one's daily life. Answer the following questions to become more aware of the cognitive distress symptoms in your life.

1. **During the past two weeks, which common cognitive distress symptoms have you experienced?**

2. **Which of these cognitive distress symptoms do you experience most frequently and repeatedly over the long run?**

3. **What stressors tend to precipitate these symptoms?**

EXERCISE 6.9
• Monitoring Your Behavioral Distress Symptoms

Behavioral distress symptoms can be a direct or indirect reflection of internal tension. Direct behavioral distress symptoms occur with little conscious effort (e.g., being easily startled, talking faster than usual, and getting easily side-tracked from projects) and directly reflect internal tension. Indirect behavioral distress symptoms require more of a conscious effort (e.g., increased smoking or alcohol consumption and use of illegal drugs) and they are used to release internal tension. Unfortunately, indirect behavioral distress symptoms often lead to more distress because they are destructive by nature. Answer the following questions to become more aware of the behavioral distress symptoms in your life.

1. **During the past two weeks, which common behavioral distress symptoms have you experienced?**

2. **Which of these behavioral distress symptoms do you experience most frequently and repeatedly over the long run?**

3. **What stressors tend to precipitate these symptoms?**

Harcourt, Inc.

EXERCISE 6.10
• Monitoring Your Physical Distress Symptoms

Physical distress symptoms are often the most visible, therefore they are the easiest to monitor. How you move and hold your body conveys a great deal about your internal tension. Answer the following questions to become more aware of the physical distress symptoms in your life.

1. **During the past two weeks, which common physical distress symptoms have you experienced?**

2. **Which of these physical distress symptoms do you experience most frequently and repeatedly over the long run?**

3. **What stressors tend to precipitate these symptoms?**

Harcourt, Inc.

CHAPTER 6 SELF-TEST

Instructions: Circle true or false. Answers can be found in the appendix.

1. Anxiety, depression, and fear only affect one's emotional well-being.
   True   **False**

2. Sadness is often referred to as the "common cold" of emotional disorders.
   True   **False**

3. Anger most often is a secondary emotion.
   True   **False**

4. Regular aerobic exercise has been shown to be very effective in reducing depression.
   True   **False**

5. Thoughts such as "should have," "could have," and "would have" tend to cause anxiety.
   True   **False**

6. When people feel shame, they usually try to make amends because they have done something wrong.
   True   **False**

7. A nervous breakdown refers to a breakdown of one's nerves or nervous system.
   True   **False**

8. Fuzzy thinking, forgetfulness, and nightmares are all examples of behavioral distress symptoms.
   True   **False**

9. Irritability, withdrawal, and being easily startled are indirect behavioral distress symptoms.
   True   **False**

10. A person cannot experience emotional, cognitive, physical, and behavioral distress symptoms all at one time.
    True   **False**

Application Exercises for CHAPTER 7: Distress-Related Symptoms

EXERCISE 7.1

• Solving The Health Care Problem

Most people would agree that we have a definite health care problem in our country. There are too many people who do not have access to health care (in either form of prevention or treatment). Using the information in Chapter 7 on the supply-side and demand-side approaches to health-care reform, write a brief essay below considering the following questions:

- **What suggestions do you have that would ensure all Americans access to adequate health care?**
- **How can medical care costs be controlled and contained?**
- **What specific programs or social policies could be implemented that would motivate Americans to make more positive, health-enhancing lifestyle choices, therefore decreasing the incidence of illness and disease?**
- **How might our country pay for the additional programs and health care costs?**

EXERCISE 7.2
• Taking A Personal Look At The Links Between Stress And Illness

Stress is related to disease and illness in four ways:

1. By imposing long-term wear and tear on the mind and body.
2. By directly causing a disease or illness.
3. By aggravating an existing illness or disease.
4. By altering health habits.

Considering these four links between stress and disease, give at least one example for each link that either you have personally experienced or someone close to you has experienced.

Link #1 (long-term wear and tear)

    Example of disease/illness:

    How could you (or the person close to you) have prevented or reduced the severity of this disease or illness?

Link #2 (directly causing)

    Example of disease/illness:

    How could you (or the person close to you) have prevented or reduced the severity of this disease or illness?

Link #3 (aggravating)

    Example of disease/illness:

    How could you (or the person close to you) have prevented or reduced the severity of this disease or illness?

Link #4 (altering health habits)

    Example of disease/illness:

    How could you (or the person close to you) have prevented or reduced the severity of this disease or illness?

Harcourt, Inc.

EXERCISE 7.3
• Cardiovascular Disease Risk Assessment

Because cardiovascular disease continues to be our nation's number one killer, it is important to realize that everyone is a potential victim. Complete the following assessment, adapted from the American Heart Association, to determine your risk factors for developing cardiovascular disease.

RISK FACTORS YOU <u>CANNOT</u> CONTROL.

1. **Do you have a family history of premature coronary heart disease (definite heart attack or sudden death before 55 years of age in father or other immediate male relative, or before 65 years of age in mother or other immediate female relative)?**

    YES   NO

• A family history of premature coronary heart disease is an important risk factor.

2. **Are you a male 45 years or older? Female 55 years or older? Or a female experiencing premature menopause without estrogen replacement therapy?**

    YES   NO

• It should not surprise you that as a person gets older, the risk for cardiovascular disease increases due to wear and tear on the body. But take heart because by making positive lifestyle choices, you can have a strong, healthy heart when you are 80 or 90. Cardiovascular disease is not an inevitable consequence of aging.
• When a woman experiences premature menopause, low density lipoprotein (LDL) cholesterol (the "bad cholesterol") levels rise more rapidly, possibly because of the loss of estrogen (the primary female hormone).

3. **Are your ancestors of African American descent?**   **YES   NO**

• African-Americans are more likely to develop certain types of cardiovascular diseases (e.g., high blood pressure and strokes) when compared to whites. Researchers are unable to identify a specific variable for this difference. Some researchers suggest poverty, family history, lifestyle, diet, and stress may play a role.

4. **Are you a male?**   **YES   NO**

• Men have a higher risk of cardiovascular disease than women, particularly before age 50. Women tend to develop cardiovascular disease about a decade later than men due to the protective effect of the female sex hormone, estrogen. Estrogen has been shown to increase high density lipoprotein (HDL) cholesterol ("the good guys") and decreasing the harmful LDL levels.

RISK FACTORS YOU <u>CAN</u> CONTROL.

1. **Do you currently smoke?**   **YES   NO**

• The Surgeon General has declared that smoking is the most dangerous risk factor for cardiovascular disease because nicotine overstimulates the heart and increases blood clotting, carbon monoxide decreases cardiovascular efficiency, and tar damages coronary arteries which makes it easier for cholesterol to build up. A major reduction in cardiovascular disease risk occurs even within the first year after a person stops smoking.

2. **Do you have high blood pressure (Over 140/90 mm Hg)?**   **YES   NO**

• Having your blood pressure checked is the easiest way to monitor your risk for cardiovascular disease because as blood pressure goes up, so does the risk of cardiovascular disease. High blood pressure, or hypertension, forces the heart to pump harder than normal.

Harcourt, Inc.

3. Do you exercise less than three times a week?   YES   NO

• Regular exercise reduces the risk of cardiovascular disease in several ways: the heart becomes more efficient in delivering oxygen to working muscles, desirable body weight can be maintained or unwanted body weight can be lost, and blood pressure is lowered.

4a. Is your cholesterol level over 200 mg/dl?   YES   NO

• The measurement of cholesterol in the blood is one of the most reliable indicators of the formation of plaque buildup on the inner walls of the arteries. A large number of studies support a direct relationship between an elevated cholesterol level and the rate of cardiovascular disease. For every 1% drop in blood cholesterol, studies show a 2% reduction in heart attack risk.

b. Is your HDL cholesterol level (the "good" cholesterol) less than 35 mg/dl?

          YES   NO

• Although total cholesterol level is an important risk factor for cardiovascular disease, the specific number of HDLs and LDLs is also important. Higher HDL cholesterol levels appear to offer a protection against coronary heart disease, particularly if HDL levels are greater than 60mg/dl. Some researchers believe HDLs actually decrease the plaque accumulation on the artery walls by taking the cholesterol in the blood to the liver where it is metabolized.

c. Is your LDL cholesterol level (the "bad" cholesterol) greater than 130 mg/dl?

          YES   NO

• A direct relationship exists between LDL levels and the rate of cardiovascular disease. LDLs are actually a component of the plaque formation in the arteries. LDL levels should be less than 130 mg/dl.

5. Is your diet high in saturated fats (animal products)?   YES   NO

• All animal products contain both saturated fat (the "worst" type of fat) and cholesterol. On the other hand, plant products are generally low in saturated fat and contain no cholesterol. Therefore, your daily diet should primarily consist of plant products (complex carbohydrates, vegetables, and fruit) and animal products should be consumed in moderation.

6. Is your diet high in triglycerides (e.g., sugar, alcohol, and refined sugars)?

          YES   NO

• Triglyceride levels tend to be highest in those whose diets are high in calories, sugar, alcohol, and refined starches. High levels of these fats may increase the risk of obesity, but cutting back on these foods can reduce high triglyceride levels.

7. Do you have diabetes?   YES   NO

• Diabetes, whether insulin dependent or non-insulin dependent, increases the risk for cardiovascular disease. Reasons for this increased risk are not entirely clear.

8. Do you often experience easily-aroused hostility?   YES   NO

• Researchers have found that people who experience hostility frequently are more vulnerable to heart disease probably due to increased blood pressure, increased free-fatty acids and cholesterol in the bloodstream, and increased cardiac output.

9. Are you overweight?   YES   NO

• Excessive body fat (weight) is unhealthy for the heart because the excess weight makes the heart work harder. When excessive body fat is stored around the abdominal region, rather than the hips and buttocks, there is even a greater risk of coronary heart disease because of the additional strain on the heart.

The more questions you answered "yes" to, the higher your risk of developing coronary heart disease in the future. Using a separate piece of paper, write a brief essay describing specific lifestyle changes you could make to decrease your risk.

Harcourt, Inc.

EXERCISE 7.4
• Monitoring Blood Pressure

During the next month, have your blood pressure taken at least four times and record the readings. You can do this using public blood-pressure machines at a pharmacy, supermarket, or mall, at a drop-in clinic, with assistance from an acquaintance from a medical field, or for a modest amount you can purchase and use your own blood pressure kit. Record your blood pressure readings--as well as other information about factors such as emotional stress, fatigue, the presence of disease or illness, current health habits (i.e., smoking, caffeine or alcohol consumption, and drug use) or recent physical exertion that might have influenced these readings.

Date and Time	Blood Pressure Reading	Comments

EXERCISE 7.5
• Headaches And Stress

If you or someone close to you suffers from headaches, use the questions below to better understand the relationship between headaches and stress.

1. **What were the headache symptoms?**

2. **Were there indicators that the body was fatigued or distressed to increase the likelihood of the headache?**

3. **What circumstances, events, pressures, or distressors might have contributed to the headache?**

4. **Looking back, how might stress have been managed differently to reduce the risk of a headache developing or decrease the severity of the headache?**

Harcourt, Inc.

CHAPTER 7 SELF-TEST

Instructions: Circle true or false. Answers can be found in the appendix.

1. The supply-side approach to health care reform emphasizes prevention rather than treatment.
    True   **False**

2. Psychoneuroimmunology is a new scientific field that brings together the study of the mind, the central nervous system, and the immune system.
    True   **False**

3. A blood pressure reading of 140/90 is referred to as normal blood pressure.
    True   **False**

4. The term referring to the amount of pressure on the inside walls of blood vessels at the moment of heart beat (contraction) is diastolic blood pressure.
    True   **False**

5. LDLs (low density lipoproteins) are the "good guys" because they discard cholesterol to the liver.
    True   **False**

6. Malignant tumors are often fatal because of their ability to metastasize.
    True   **False**

7. Rheumatoid arthritis is a result of long term wear and tear on the joints.
    True   **False**

8. Migraine headaches and coronary artery disease resemble one another in that both are problems of the vascular system.
    True   **False**

9. Recent evidence strongly suggests that stress is the dominant cause of peptic ulcers.
    True   **False**

10. Chronic insomnia is the type of insomnia when a person can't fall asleep.
    True   **False**

Application Exercises for CHAPTER 8:
Type A Behavior and Hostility

EXERCISE 8.1
• Personalizing Mr. A And Mr. B

Using the typical daily schedules of Mr. A and Mr. B, as described in "One Day in the Life of Mr. A and Mr. B" (Chapter 8), and the questions below, look for comparisons between yourself and Mr. A and Mr. B.

1. To what extent can you identify with the experiences of Mr. A and Mr. B?

2. What specific similarities do you see between characteristics of Mr. A and Mr. B, on one hand, and yourself, on the other?

3. From this comparison, what do you see about yourself that you would like to change. Be specific.

EXERCISE 8.2
• Effect Of Social Environment In Display Of The Type A Pattern

The presence of Type A behavior depends on the combination of personality disposition and social environment. For example, when an organization is fast-paced or chronically overloaded, or when it encourages chronic time urgency, then a Type A-disposed person is more likely to act and think Type A. The same person in a more tranquil setting may not seem Type A at all. With this in mind, answer the questions below concerning specific circumstances in which your Type A tendencies were more and less brought out.

1. **Briefly describe the social environment (i.e., family, school, work, and fraternity/sorority) that had a tendency to bring out your Type A characteristics. What was it about these circumstances that you believe elicited your Type A behavior.**

2. **Briefly describe the social environment (i.e., family, school, work, and fraternity/sorority) that had a tendency to bring out your Type B characteristics. What was it about these circumstances that you believe elicited your Type B behavior.**

EXERCISE 8.3
• Effects Of Type A Behavior On Quality Of Life

In Chapter 8 you read about a number of variables (personal qualities and experiences) that were correlated with Type A behavior. Thinking of your own observations and experiences, you are invited to answer the following questions about the impact of Type A behavior on yourself and others you know. Use the list of variables given under the "Quality of Life" heading in Chapter 8 as a guide for your writing.

1. **What specific aspects of your quality of life do you think your Type A pattern has negatively affected (e.g., your moods, your performance, your relationships with others, your energy level, and your health)? See if you can describe exactly how your Type A pattern has impacted these outcomes.**

2. **Now think of someone you know quite well. What specific aspects of his or her quality of life has been negatively affected by Type A pattern characteristics? Again, see if you can describe exactly how this person's Type A tendencies had these effects.**

EXERCISE 8.4
• Are You Hostile?

Hostility has been shown to be the most toxic element of Type A behavior because it has been linked to premature death and a low quality of wellness. Complete the following hostility scale to see if hostility is decreasing your wellness and increasing your chances of premature death. Answer as honestly as possible.

	True	False
You think most people would lie to get ahead.		
Most people make friends because friends are likely to be useful to them.		
Some members of your family have habits that annoy you very much.		
You are easily angered.		
At times you have had to be rough with people who were rude or annoying.		
You are often inclined to go out of your way to win a point with someone who has opposed you.		
Give yourself one point for each true answer and two points for each false answer, then add your score. See Exercise 8.5 to compare and assess your score.		

Source: Gallup Poll (1994). Scale developed by Redford Williams from Cook & Medley (1954).

EXERCISE 8.5
• Comparing and Assessing Your Hostility Score

Below is the distribution of scores on the six-item hostility scale shown in Exercise 8.4 among 277 undergraduate students.

Mean: 9.3
Median: 9.0
Distribution:

SCORE	PERCENTAGE OF RESPONDENTS
6 OR 7	10
8	19
9	27
10	24
11 or 12	20
	100%

1. How does your score compare?

2. How satisfied are you with your scores? Why?

3. If your score is higher than you would like, using Williams's "Tips for Reducing Hostility" in Chapter 10 as a guide, what might you do--starting today?

EXERCISE 8.6
• Managing Type A Behavior

Use the following tips for managing Type A behavior that are discussed in Chapter 8 to write a brief essay describing which of these tips would be helpful for you (or someone close to you) in managing Type A behavior. Be specific.

Tip #1: Review your successes.

Tip #2: Believe in your ability to change.

Tip #3: Enter into a thorough self-appraisal.

Tip #4: Retrieve your total personality.

Tip #5: Make gestures toward myth, ritual, and tradition.

CHAPTER 8 SELF-TEST

Instructions: Circle true or false. Answers can be found in the appendix.

1.   Family and friends are the two major influences that shape personality.

     True   **False**

2.   The Type A in the Type A personality patterns stands for Anger.
     True   **False**

3.   The idea that emotions, such as anger, negatively affect the heart is a new one.
     True   **False**

4.   Hyperaggressiveness is the most toxic element of Type A behavior.
     True   **False**

5.   Type As often possess a drive toward self-destruction.
     True   **False**

6.   There are positive benefits of some elements of Type A behavior.
     True   **False**

7.   Type A is a risk factor for heart disease.
     True   **False**

8.   Type A behavior cannot be successfully changed.
     True   **False**

9.   One's social environment has little influence on Type A behavior.
     True   **False**

10. Anger, irritation, aggravation, and impatience are all components of free-floating hostility.
     True   **False**

Application Exercises for CHAPTER 9: Distress-Prone Personality Patterns

EXERCISE 9.1

• Assessing Your Procrastination

Most procrastinators would argue, "I work better under pressure" or "I enjoy the rush of doing something at the last minute." Yet, the quality of work often is decreased when one procrastinates. Some studies have shown that procrastinators are sick more often and visit health care practitioners more than their non-procrastinating peers. Positive stress can help to motivate us to meet deadlines, but that's not procrastination. Use the following questions to assess your procrastination habits.

1. **To what extent do you procrastinate? Are there certain areas of your life in which you procrastinate more than others?**

2. **What personal beliefs contribute to your procrastination? What personal beliefs prevent procrastination?**

3. **What are some examples of your self-talk statements when you procrastinate? When you don't procrastinate?**

4. **How does procrastination affect your wellness? How does your procrastination affect others in your life? If you don't have a tendency to procrastinate, explain how avoiding procrastination decreases the amount of distress you experience.**

Harcourt, Inc.

EXERCISE 9.2
• Assessing Your Type E Qualities

Even though the Type E pattern was originally designed for women, it can also apply to men in our society. Using the following questions, assess your Type E qualities.

1. Which Type E beliefs, discussed in Chapter 9, characterize your own thinking?

2. Is your daily life affected by any Type E beliefs and behavior? Are others around you affected?

3. Rewrite your personal Type E beliefs to make them more helpful and realistic.

4. What concrete differences would occur in your life if you were to apply these rewritten alternative, more reasonable beliefs?

5. What specific decisions and actions can you take to implement these new beliefs?

EXERCISE 9.3
• Are You A Worry Wart?

It is not uncommon to be a worrier in our society. From sociological influences, like the media and early messages from our parents, it's understandable why worrying is so prevalent in people's lives today. Use the assessment below to realize what situations you really have control over. If you can't control it, you shouldn't worry about it. Spend your time and energy on the things you can control.

	Always	Sometimes	Rarely
I spend a lot of time worrying about what will happen in my future.			
When things are going well for me, I worry about when something bad will happen.			
I believe worrying about people in my life is a good way to show them I care.			
I worry about the next day's events when I'm lying in bed at night.			
I worry that I'll be involved in either a bike or car accident when I'm either biking or driving.			
Dying is something that I worry about.			
I worry about my health.			
I worry about the health of my loved ones.			
In intimate relationships, I worry that my partner will stop loving me.			
I spend a lot of time worrying about my finances.			

1. Make a personal list of current worries in your life.

2. Cross out the items on your list that you have no control over. Remember to try to let the uncontrollable situations in your life go. For the remaining items, write down specific self-talk statements that you use.

3. Are your self-talk statements concerning your worries realistic or justified? How could you change your current self-talk to minimize the amount of time you spend worrying?

Harcourt, Inc.

EXERCISE 9.4
• The Addiction-Prone Pattern

Answer the questions below for a better understanding of the addiction-prone pattern in general and how it may specifically affect your wellness.

1. For years, scientists have tried to explain why some people become addicted and others do not. What factors do you think contribute to a person possessing addiction-prone characteristics?

2. Do you or someone you know possess certain addiction-prone characteristics? Which ones? What factors contributed to these characteristics?

3. How do addiction-prone characteristics negatively affect one's wellness?

EXERCISE 9.5
• The Codependent Pattern

Answer the questions below for a better understanding of the codependent pattern in general and how it may specifically affect your wellness.

1. Research has shown that more women than men possess codependent characteristics. What do you think are the reasons for this gender difference?

2. Do you or someone you know possess certain codependent characteristics? Which ones? What factors contributed to these characteristics?

3. How do codependent characteristics negatively affect one's wellness?

EXERCISE 9.6
• Creating Your Own Distress-Prone Personality Pattern

Using specific distress-prone characteristics that you and/or people you know possess, describe a new distress-prone personality pattern. You may use characteristics from any of the personality patterns discussed in Chapter 9 or use other characteristics that weren't mentioned. Be sure to list specific characteristics that completely describe this new distress-prone personality pattern you are creating and give it a name.

CHAPTER 9 SELF-TEST

Instructions: Circle true or false. Answers can be found in the appendix.

1. The two types of perfectionists described in Chapter 9 are major and minor perfectionists.
    True   **False**

2. Perfectionists are usually very productive and creative individuals.
    True   **False**

3. Being preoccupied with "shoulds," engaging in all-or-nothing thinking, and overgeneralizing are common characteristics of a procrastinator.
    True   **False**

4. The Type E pattern is influenced by sociological and psychological factors.
    True   **False**

5. Worriers are creative, caring, and intelligent people.
    True   **False**

6. People sometimes learn to become helpless when faced with repeated uncontrollable events.
    True   **False**

7. Learned pessimism includes the tendency to interpret bad events as externally caused, temporary, and specific.
    True   **False**

8. Addictions are a result of an interplay of personality style, brain biology, and social influences.
    True   **False**

9. Caretaking, low self-esteem, weak boundaries, and controlling are all characteristics of the addiction-prone personality pattern.
    True   **False**

10. Most of the distress-prone personality patterns are also considered distress-seeking patterns.
    True   **False**

Application Exercises for CHAPTER 10: Distress-Resistant Personality Patterns

EXERCISE 10.1
• Maximizing Your Type B Qualities

A lot of people falsely believe that Type B's are lazy and underachievers, when in actuality, Type B's are often more productive because they can delegate easier and they aren't constantly struggling with time. Use the following questions to assess your current Type B qualities and how you might expand upon them.

1. I currently possess the following Type B qualities:

2. Type B qualities that I would like to strengthen or acquire include:

3. What benefits might you receive if you possessed more Type B qualities? Would others in your life benefit as well from these changes?

EXERCISE 10.2
• Practice Seeing The Glasses In Your Life As Half-Full vs. Half-Empty

Being optimistic can have a significant positive impact on one's wellness. Over the next couple of days, become more aware of your self talk in everyday situations. Use the table below to write down the specific situations in which you normally use optimism and situations in which you normally use pessimism. When you catch yourself using pessimism, write down the pessimistic self-talk statement and then rewrite it, changing it into an optimistic self-talk statement. At first your revised comments might sound a bit "corny." But that's probably due to the fact that most people are accustomed to using pessimistic self-talk. Eventually, your optimistic self-talk will become more natural to use.

OPTIMISTIC SELF-TALK

Situation	Optimistic Self-Talk Statement

PESSIMISTIC SELF-TALK

Situation	Pessimistic Self-Talk Statement	Rewritten Self-Talk Statement

Harcourt, Inc.

EXERCISE 10.3
• Taking A Closer Look At Sense Of Coherence

The sense of coherence personality pattern has the following three main components:

1. **Comprehensibility** - Believing that the events in your life are not chaotic, random, or accidental. Believing there is a reason behind the events that occur in your life.
2. **Manageability** - Believing that you possess resources (both internally or externally) to meet the demands in your life.
3. **Meaningfulness** - Believing that the demands in your life are worth responding to and that those demands are seen as challenges, opportunities for personal growth.

Write a brief essay considering the following questions:
• **Which components of the sense of coherence theory do you possess?**
• **What factors have led to the development of these components in your life?**
• **What effect do these components have on your life?**
• **Briefly describe how the spiritual dimension of wellness is related to the sense of coherence theory.**

EXERCISE 10.4
• How Resilient Are You?

Resiliency, the ability to recover from illness, disease, depression, or any other adversity, has long been used to describe good mental health. Mental health experts suggest that resiliency is the key characteristic that distinguishes between the mentally healthy and unhealthy. It's not that mentally healthy people never experience distress, they just possess the ability to bounce back within a reasonable amount of time. Assess your current resiliency using the exercise below.

	Always	Sometimes	Never
I can easily laugh at myself and find the humor in everyday situations.			
I consider myself a creative person.			
When I make mistakes, I see them as an opportunity for personal growth and challenge.			
I am flexible when things in my life don't go as expected.			
I am a curious person who asks questions.			
I am a good problem-solver.			
I am an independent person.			

1. Which resiliency qualities, mentioned above, would you like to strengthen or acquire?

2. What benefits might you receive if you were more resilient?

3. Why do you think resiliency has so many positive affects on a person's wellness, wealth, happiness, and longevity?

Harcourt, Inc.

EXERCISE 10.5
• Are You A Survivor?

In studying survivors, Walter and Siebert (1999) have discovered that there are key characteristics that the majority of survivors possess, such as biphasic traits, serendipity, synergy, self-actualization, creativity, intuition, humor, and competence under pressure. Answer the questions below to assess which survivor characteristics you currently possess and which ones you could benefit from. (See Chapter 9 for a more detailed description of each of these characteristics.)

1. **Which specific personality traits do you possess that enable you to "survive"? Give at least two examples in which these traits have helped you "survive" some event in your life.**

2. **Which survivor personality traits would you like to acquire or strengthen? How might you make these desired traits part of your personality?**

EXERCISE 10.6
• A Closer Look At The Type C Pattern

The Type C model is based on the Type C experience, where everything seems to flow naturally at a very high level of performance. The "C" in this model stands for three C's in the Type C pattern: challenge, confidence, and control. Using what you read in Chapter 10 about the Type C pattern, answer the following questions.

1. **Give examples that explain how the Type C pattern draws some of the best attributes from the Type A and Type B patterns.**

2. **Describe times in your own life when you have experienced the panic zone, the drone zone, and the C zone. What were the circumstances? How did it feel? What were the consequences for yourself and others?**

Harcourt, Inc.

EXERCISE 10.7
• Self-Talk And Self-Worth: Your Reactions

Consider the following interrelated points about self-talk and self-worth. Indicate whether you agree or disagree with the point made and give specific examples of how it may apply to you.

INTERRELATED POINTS ABOUT SELF-TALK AND SELF-WORTH.	AGREE OR DISAGREE	HOW DOES THIS POINT APPLY TO ME?
I create my own inner reality.		
I deserve to create feelings of self-worth because I am a unique human being.		
My self-worth can be (even if it is not now) positive, steady, and independent of social position, accomplishments, others' opinions, and my own fallibilities.		
Because my own self-worth can exist unconditionally, it need be neither proven nor protected.		
Self-created distress associated with perfectionism, hurry sickness, anger, and anxiety often result from unnecessary struggles to prove or protect my self-worth.		
I accept responsibility for my own sense of self-worth.		

EXERCISE 10.8

• Moving Toward Greater Self-Actualization

Consider the qualities of the self-actualized person as described in Chapter 10. Write an essay below about the strengths and weaknesses of your own self-actualization and about steps you can take to move toward greater self-actualization.

EXERCISE 10.9
• Creating Your Own Distress-Resistant Personality Pattern

Using specific distress-resistant characteristics that you and/or people you know possess, describe a new distress-resistant personality pattern. You may use characteristics from any of the personality patterns discussed in Chapter 10 or use other characteristics that weren't mentioned. Be sure to list specific characteristics that completely describe this new distress-prone personality pattern you are creating and give it a name.

CHAPTER 10 SELF-TEST

Instructions: Circle true or false. Answers can be found in the appendix.

1. The main difference between Type A's and Type B's is that Type B's experience less hostility than Type A's.
    True   **False**

2. Type B's are usually unmotivated to succeed and they do not work very hard.
    True   **False**

3. The trusting heart personality pattern leads to social integration and social support.
    True   **False**

4. Learned optimism involves interpreting good events as being externally caused, temporary, and specific.
    True   **False**

5. The three C's of hardiness are challenge, confidence, and control.
    True   **False**

6. Studies clearly show that hardiness offers protection against distress and illness, especially during clustering life changes.
    True   **False**

7. The sense of coherence theory refers to the tendency of low-stress families to communicate effectively.
    True   **False**

8. The trait most often found in survivors is resiliency.
    True   **False**

9. Synergy refers to someone having a natural tendency to respond with insight and wisdom under the pressure of an accident or other misfortune.
    True   **False**

10. The Type C pattern draws some of the best attributes from the Type A and Type B patterns.
    True   **False**

Harcourt, Inc.

Application Exercises for CHAPTER 11: Distress-Provoking and Distress-Preventing Social Influences

EXERCISE 11.1
• Illustrations Of Social And Personal Change

It's important to understand the difference between social change and personal change and how they affect one another. Even though social change affects a large number of people at once, oftentimes social change will lead to personal change. Answer the following questions to better understand the concepts of social change and personal change. Remember the examples you give don't have to be negative, since change can have a positive influence on our lives.

1. **Briefly describe three examples of social changes that have directly impacted your own stress level. Did these social changes lead to personal change? Be sure to clearly illustrate the direct links between those social changes and the effects on your life.**

2. **Briefly describe several personal changes you have experienced during the past year. What were the reasons for these personal changes? Were they influenced by a social change? Describe how these personal changes affected your stress level.**

Harcourt, Inc.

EXERCISE 11.2
• Personal Experience Of Overchoice

Most people in our society can relate to stress that is created from overchoice because we usually have more than one choice when making even the simplest of decisions. One may experience overchoice by just wandering down the aisles of a supermarket. Overchoice adds to stress and distress, since every option is a stressor.

1. **List at least three examples of overchoice you have experienced lately. Next to each of your examples, indicate whether or not overchoice led to distress. (Simply write "yes" next to the examples that led to distress and "no" if it didn't.)**

   Example #1:

   Example #2:

   Example #3:

2. **How can you (or people in general) prevent overchoice from leading to distress?**

Harcourt, Inc.

EXERCISE 11.3
• Your Support Review

Schlossberg (1989) suggests there our four potential resources, the four S's, that are vital for managing change. These four S's (Your overall *Situation*, Your *Self*, Your *Supports*, and Your *Strategies* for coping) help minimize distress that can sometimes accompany transitions. Answer the questions below to analyze your *supports* during a particular transition you are currently experiencing.

1. **What specific transition are you currently experiencing in your life as a result of a change?**

2. **Are you getting what you need for this transition in terms of:**

Affect? (Emotion?)	Yes	No
Affirmation?	Yes	No
Aid?	Yes	No

3. **Do you have a range of types of support--spouse or partner, other close family or friends, co-workers/colleagues/neighbors, organizations, strangers?**

Yes	No

4. **Has your "convoy of social support"--from intimate to institution--been interrupted by this transition?**

Yes	No

5. **Do you regard your support for this transition as:**

A high resource?	Yes	No
A low resource?	Yes	No
A mixed bag?	Yes	No
Okay?	Yes	No

6. **What changes could you make in regards to your support to help minimize distress as a result of the transition you are currently experiencing?**

Source: Schlossberg (1989, 62)   Harcourt, Inc.

EXERCISE 11.4
• Coping Strategies For Transitions

Stress always accompanies transitions, but distress doesn't. To minimize distress as a result of a transition in your life, maximize your coping strategies. Schlossberg (1989) suggests a number of coping strategies that are listed below. Indicate which of the following coping strategies you are currently using and which ones you will use in the future to prevent the stress from turning into distress.

COPING STRATEGIES	NOW USE	WILL USE
TAKING ACTION TO CHANGE OR MODIFY THE TRANSITION		
Negotiating		
Taking optimistic action		
Seeking advice		
Asserting yourself		
Brainstorming a new plan		
Taking legal action (if needed)		
CHANGING THE MEANING OF THE TRANSITIONS		
Applying the knowledge of the transition process		
Rehearsing		
Developing rituals		
Making positive comparisons		
Rearranging priorities		
Relabeling or reframing		
Selectively ignoring		
Using denial		
Using humor		
Having faith		
MANAGING REACTIONS TO STRESS		
Playing		
Using relaxation skills		
Expressing emotions		
Doing physical activity		
Participating in counseling, therapy, or support groups		
Reading		
DOING NOTHING		
OTHER STRATEGIES		

Source: Schlossberg (1989, 89)   Harcourt, Inc.

EXERCISE 11.5
• Social Readjustment Rating Scale

This scale is useful for determining the clustering of life events in your own life. To use the scale, record the values (Life Change Units) corresponding to the events you have experienced during the past year. These values indicate the average stressfulness of each event on a scale of 0-100. Thus, if you have experienced one personal injury or illness in the past year, record 53. If you have experienced two personal injuries or illnesses in the past year, record 53 twice (106).

LIFE EVENT	MEAN VALUE
Death of spouse	100
Divorce	73
Marital separation from mate	65
Detention in jail or other institution	63
Death of a close family member	63
Major personal injury or illness	53
Marriage	50
Being fired at work	47
Marital reconciliation with mate	45
Retirement from work	45
Major change in health or behavior of a family member	44
Pregnancy	40
Sexual difficulties	39
Gaining new family members (through birth, adoption, elder moving in, etc.)	39
Major business readjustment (merger, reorganization, bankruptcy, etc.)	39
Major change in financial state (a lot worse or a lot better off than usual)	38
Death of a close friend	37
Changing to a different line of work	36
Major change in the number of arguments with spouse (more or fewer arguments than usual, about childrearing, personal habits, etc.)	35
Taking out a mortgage or loan for a major purchase (home, business, etc.)	31
Foreclosure on a mortgage or loan	30
Major change in responsibilities at work (promotion, demotion, lateral transfer)	29
Son or daughter leaving home (for marriage, to attend college, etc.)	29
Trouble with in-laws	29
Outstanding personal achievement	28
Spouse beginning or ceasing work outside the home	26
Beginning or ceasing formal schooling	26
Major change in living conditions (building a new home, remodeling, deterioration of home/neighborhood)	25
Revision of personal habits (dress, manners, associations, etc.)	24
Trouble with boss	23
Major change in working hours or conditions	20
Change in residence	20
Changing to a new school	20
Major change in usual type and/or amount of recreation	19
Major change in church activities (a lot more or fewer than usual)	19
Major change in social activities (clubs, dancing, movies, visiting, etc.)	18
Taking out a mortgage or loan for a lesser purchase (for a car, TV, freezer, etc.)	17
Major change in sleeping habits (a lot more or less sleep, or a change in part of day when sleep occurs)	16
Major change in number of family get-togethers (more or fewer than usual)	15
Major change in eating habits (a lot more or less food intake, or very different meal hours or surroundings)	13
Vacation	13
Christmas	12
Minor violation of the law (traffic tickets, jaywalking, disturbing the peace, etc.)	11

Source: Holmes and Rahe (1967, 213)

Add up the total number of your points: _____. **Use Exercise 11.6 to learn more about your score.**

Harcourt, Inc.

EXERCISE 11.6
• Evaluating Your Social Readjustment Scale

Answer the following questions to learn more about your social readjustment score from Exercise 11.5.

1. Were you surprised at your score? Why or why not?

2. How has the presence or absence of clustering life changes affected your wellness in the last year?

3. In the future, how might you minimize distress that is associated with clustered life changes?

EXERCISE 11.7
• Daily Hassles

When discussing daily hassles, it is important to understand two key principles. The first principle is to remember how influential one's interpretation is on determining the number of distressors a person experiences. Daily hassles are only daily hassles when they are interpreted that way. Granted, it is a lot easier to say than to do, but a person can control his or her interpretation of events. The second principle is to understand how these daily hassles or micro events can negatively affect one's wellness. Research has demonstrated that it seems to be the accumulation of daily hassles rather than large negative events that wears a person down, both mentally and physically. Considering those two principles, answer the following questions to assess how daily hassles affect your life.

1. **What are some of your daily hassles?**

2. **How are you affected by these daily hassles? Consider your emotions, physical state, relationships, productivity, or behavior.**

Now choose three daily hassles. For each one, write down your original self-talk statement that causes the demand to become a daily hassles and then re-write the self-talk statement. Once you get accustomed to using your new self-talk statement for each specific situation, that demand will no longer become a daily hassle and you can work on another three daily hassles.

DAILY HASSLE #1:

Current self-talk statement:

Revised self talk statement:

DAILY HASSLE #2:

Current self-talk statement:

Revised self talk statement:

DAILY HASSLE #3:

Current self-talk statement:

Revised self talk statement: Harcourt, Inc.

EXERCISE 11.8
• Daily Uplifts

If you focus on your daily hassles more than your daily uplifts, you aren't alone. We often become accustomed to look for the bad in everything. Minimizing the number of daily hassles you experience is a good start to minimize the amount of distress you experience, but maximizing daily uplifts will also contribute to less distress and higher levels of wellness. Use the following tools to increase your awareness of the daily uplifts you experience, but don't always recognize.

For the next few days, before you go to bed use the space below to write down at least five uplifts that you experienced during the day. Hopefully, by reflecting on these daily uplifts you'll start to recognize them more as they actually occur throughout your day.

Five uplifts I experienced today were:

Five uplifts I experienced today were:

For the next few days before you go to bed write down at least five uplifts that you will include in your daily routine. You might actually want to right the uplifts down and schedule them in, especially if you have a busy day planned. Once you notice how positively these daily uplifts influence all dimensions of your wellness, you won't have to plan them and they'll become an integral part of your daily routine.

Five uplifts I will do tomorrow include:

Five uplifts I will do tomorrow include:

Harcourt, Inc.

EXERCISE 11.9
• Assessing The Five Forms Of Alienation In Your Life

All five forms of alienation have increased in our society in response to the faster pace of life. When a person experiences any form of alienation, distress levels are increased. To learn more about your experience with the five forms of alienation answer the questions below.

1. How much do you experience each form of alienation?

	A Great Deal	Somewhat	Not Very Much
Powerlessness			
Self-Estrangement			
Isolation			
Meaninglessness			
Normlessness			

2. If you do experience one or more forms of alienation, why do you think this is so? Refer to your past, your present circumstances, and to your way of viewing things (your beliefs, self-talk, and interpretations).

3. What might you do in your behavior and thinking to reduce alienation in your life? Be specific.

EXERCISE 11.10
• Distress-Prone And Distress-Resistant Workplaces

The average adult spends a large percentage of his or her time at work, so it's no wonder how a workplace can either minimize or maximize distress. Workplaces are a strong social influence on an individual's level of distress. Using personal experience and knowledge of stress management skills, create an ideal workplace that would minimize distress for employees. Consider the following questions:

1. **What specific qualities of a distress-prone work environment have you experienced?**

2. **What specific qualities of a distress-resistant work environment have you experienced?**

3. **What specific qualities would the ideal distress-resistant work environment possess?**

CHAPTER 11 SELF-TEST

Instructions: Circle true or false. Answers can be found in the appendix.

1. Sociological imagination refers to the ability to visualize positive future outcomes in your relationships.
    True   **False**

2. Attributing personal distress entirely to internal causes is known as blaming the victim.
    True   **False**

3. Jill Reiser moves from Sacramento to Chico. This illustrates social change.
    True   **False**

4. Seligman suggests the rate of depression has decreased as a result of new technology.
    True   **False**

5. The number, variety, and intensity of stressors a person experiences per day, week, or year is referred to as his or her pace of life.
    True   **False**

6. The three types of transitions that stand out as especially significant for many people are losing a loved one, changing jobs, and developing an illness or disease.
    True   **False**

7. Research among CSU, Chico athletes demonstrated the more numerous the life changes during the year preceding the season, the greater the number and severity of injuries.
    True   **False**

8. Research has shown that large negative events, such as losing a job, wear an individual down more, both mentally and physically, than daily hassles.
    True   **False**

9. When a person believes that socially unapproved behaviors are necessary and justified to achieve one's goals, he or she is experiencing the self-estrangement form of alienation.
    True   **False**

10. Cultures of wellness are good examples of distress-preventing social influences.
    True   **False**

Application Exercises for CHAPTER 12: Your Coping Response

EXERCISE 12.1
• Illustrating Stages Of Coping

In Chapter 12 you read about three stages of coping that a person goes through when experiencing a difficult situation.   First, a person engages in primary appraisal to decide whether the situation is worth being concerned about.   Secondly, a person engages in secondary appraisal to assess his or her resources for dealing with the stressor.   Lastly, a person copes, taking whatever action seems appropriate.   As a means of increasing your awareness of each stage, keep a log of two experiences during the next day or so using the format below.

1. **Stressor or Distressor:**
   Event #1:

   Event #2:

2. **Primary Appraisal** (To what degree was the event meaningful to you? Potentially threatening?)
   Event #1:

   Event #2:

3. **Secondary Appraisal** (What were your personal and environmental resources for dealing with this event?)
   Event #1:

   Event #2:

4. **Coping** (How, specifically, did you cope? What actions or mental steps did you take?)
   Event #1:

   Event #2:

5. **Results** (What consequences occurred as the result of your coping--for you and others?)
   Event #1:

   Event #2:

Harcourt, Inc.

EXERCISE 12.2
• Assessment Of Coping Resources And Constraints

Using the section in Chapter 12 on coping resources and constraints as a guide, make a list of your own internal and environmental coping resources and constraints.

1. **Coping resources:**

2. **Coping restraints:**

3. **What can you learn from this exercise? What will you do to improve your coping resources? To deal effectively with coping constraints?**

Harcourt, Inc.

EXERCISE 12.3
• Adaptive And Maladaptive Coping Patterns

Adaptive coping habits are those that enable you to deal effectively with stressful events and to minimize distress for you and others. Maladaptive coping habits are those that are ineffective in handling stressors and/or that result in unnecessary distress for self or others. In the spaces below, list as many coping habits of each type as you can.

1. **My adaptive coping habits include:**

2. **My maladaptive coping habits include:**

EXERCISE 12.4
• Trying Out Your Coping Options

Use the table below to learn more about which coping options you use. During the next two days, explain the stressors that you experience, specify which coping option you used, and whether the outcome was adaptive or maladaptive. See the example below to help get you started.

STRESSOR	COPING OPTION	OUTCOME
There is a lot of miscommunication in my workplace.	Problem-focused coping: I put communication problem on agenda for our next staff meeting.	Adaptive

Harcourt, Inc.

EXERCISE 12.5
• Assessing And Applying The Schafer Coping Model

Looking at the various options in the Schafer coping model below, what are strengths and weaknesses in your own coping style. (For more information on the Schafer coping model refer to Chapter 12.)

Alter the Stressor	Adapt to the Stressor	Avoid the Stressor
• Seeking to change a specific situation. • Changing a physical stressor. • Pacing myself and my stressor better. • Spacing my life changes better. • Increasing challenges in my life (if the problem is boredom). • Asking someone to alter his or her behavior. • Organizing time better.	• Manage self-talk. • Control physical stress response. • Manage actions. • Maintain health buffers. • Utilize available coping resources. • Avoid maladaptive reactions to distress.	• Is it best for me to avoid or withdraw from this stressor? • What would be the gains and costs? • Have all other options been exhausted?

1.   **My strengths include:**

2.   **My weaknesses include:**

3.   **What steps will you take during the next two weeks to improve upon your weaknesses in coping style?**

Harcourt, Inc.

EXERCISE 12.6
• Are You A Problem Drinker?
Use the assessment below to analyze your drinking behavior.

Section One	Yes	No
Do you occasionally drink heavily after a disappointment, a quarrel, or when the boss gives you a hard time?		
When you have trouble or feel under pressure, do you always drink more heavily than usual?		
Have you noticed that you are able to handle more liquor than you did when you were first drinking?		
Did you ever wake up on the morning after and discover that you could not remember part of the evening before, even though your friends tell you that you did not pass out?		
When drinking with other people, do you try to have a few extra drinks when others will not know about it?		
Are there certain occasions when you feel uncomfortable if alcohol is not available?		
Have you recently noticed that when you begin drinking you are in more of a hurry to get the first drink than you used to be?		
Do you sometimes feel guilty about your drinking?		

Section Two	Yes	No
Are you secretly irritated when your family or friends discuss your drinking?		
Have you recently noticed an increase in the frequency of your memory blackouts?		
Do you often wish to continue drinking after your friends say they have had enough?		
Do you usually have a reason for the occasions when you drink heavily?		
When you are sober, do you often regret things you have done or said while drinking?		
Have you tried switching brands or following different plans for controlling your drinking?		
Have you often failed to keep the promises you have made to yourself about controlling or cutting down on your drinking?		
Have you ever tried to control your drinking by making a change in jobs or moving to a new location?		
Do you try to avoid family or close friends while you are drinking?		
Are you having an increasing number of financial and work problems?		
Do more people seem to be treating you unfairly without good reason?		
Do you eat very little or irregularly when you are drinking?		
Do you sometimes have the shakes in the morning and find that it helps to have a drink?		

Section Three	Yes	No
Have you recently noticed that you cannot drink as much as you once did?		
Do you sometimes stay drunk for several days at a time?		
Do you sometimes feel very depressed and wonder whether life is worth living?		
Sometimes after periods of drinking, do you see or hear things that aren't there?		
Do you get terribly frightened after you have been drinking heavily?		

If you answered "yes" to two or more questions in any of these three sections, the National Council on Alcoholism urges you to re-evaluate your drinking behavior. Each section focuses on a more advanced stage of problem drinking.

Section One: **Early stage--drinking is a regular part of your life.**

Section Two: **Middle stage--you are having trouble controlling when, where, and how much to drink.**

Section Three: **Advanced stage--you can no longer control your desire to drink.**

Source: National Council on Alcoholism (1992)

Harcourt, Inc.

EXERCISE 12.7
• Social Norms And Drinking

A key problem with alcohol use is that in many subcultures heavy use of alcohol is supported as acceptable coping behavior--social norms that receive strong support from alcohol advertisements. Closely related is the social norm equating "a good time" or "partying" with heavy drinking. Write a brief essay using the questions below to learn more about how social norms influence your drinking behavior.

• **What social norms (shared expectations regarding do's and don'ts) exist among one or two groups to which you belong regarding alcohol consumption? Specifically, what is expected regarding: When to drink? What to drink? With whom to drink? How much to drink?**

• **What other behaviors are expected in association with drinking?**

• **How much do you believe you are influenced by these social norms?**

EXERCISE 12.8
• Reactions To Albert Mitchell's Letter

Respond to Albert Mitchell's letter to the editor in Chapter 12 concerning the drug problem in our country by writing a brief essay. Consider the following questions:

- **In what ways do you agree and disagree with Albert Mitchell's letter to the editor?**
- **In what ways do you think he is right and wrong?**
- **What points do you believe he misses, if any?**

EXERCISE 12.9
• Monitoring Your Reactions To Distress

The goal of stress management is two fold. The first goal is to learn how to successfully manage stress to minimize distress and maximize eustress. The second goal is to learn how to positively react to distress when it does occur. Use the assessment below to learn more about how you react to the distress in your life. Indicate how often you have used each of the following methods of trying to reduce your physical and emotional tension during the past six months.

	Never	Rarely	Sometimes	Often
Drink alcoholic beverages				
Smoke				
Take a tranquilizer, sleeping pill, or other prescribed medication				
Take aspirin				
Take an over-the-counter relaxant				
Drink coffee, cola, or tea				
Overeat and/or undereat				
Yell, hurt, or otherwise take it out on someone else				
Forget about it and keep going				
Use television, books, or something else to "escape" for awhile				
Take a leisurely walk				
Grin and bear it				
Redefine the situation more positively in your mind				
Change your approach to the person or stressor				
Exercise				
Do deep relaxation				
Do a breathing or muscle relaxation technique				
Talk it over with somebody				
Pray				
Use humor				
Take a day off or a vacation				

Using a separate piece of paper, write a brief essay describing how satisfied you are with your responses. Consider the following questions:
• Do you use more adaptive or maladaptive coping?
• How can you increase your adaptive coping and minimize your maladaptive coping?
• Which methods would you like to use less often? more often?

Harcourt, Inc.

CHAPTER 12 SELF-TEST

Instructions: Circle true or false. Answers can be found in the appendix.

1. Coping is a stable, relatively unchanging pattern of dealing with stressors.
    True   **False**

2. Social support, exercise, and problem-solving skills are all examples of coping resources.
    True   **False**

3. According to the three stage coping model discussed in Chapter 12, when you assess your resources for dealing with a stressor, you are engaged in primary appraisal.
    True   **False**

4. A person's life script can limit one's coping style.
    True   **False**

5. Jeff tends to respond to pressure much like he remembered his dad doing when Jeff was a child. This is an example of a deliberate coping response.
    True   **False**

6. Adaptive coping, also known as positive coping, contributes to wellness.
    True   **False**

7. Organizing time more effectively during final exam week is an example of emotion-focused coping.
    True   **False**

8. Hardiness is likely to lead to regressive coping.
    True   **False**

9. According to the Schafer coping model, the three As of adaptive coping are alter, adapt, and avoid the stressor.
    True   **False**

10. A key problem with using alcohol as a coping option in our society is that in many subcultures heavy use of alcohol is supported as acceptable coping behavior.
    True   **False**

Harcourt, Inc.

Application Exercises for CHAPTER 13: Health Buffers

EXERCISE 13.1
• Benefits Of Regular Exercise

There are over a hundred proven benefits of regular exercise. Using the list below and personal experience, answer the questions on the following page to take a closer look at your benefits of a regular exercise program and how they affect stress.

Benefits of Regular Exercise

- Reduce Depression
- Increase Energy
- Increase Optimism
- Increase Mental Flexibility
- Relieves Stress
- Prevents Bound Energy (Distress)
- Reduces Risk Of Osteoporosis
- Reduces Risk Of Cancer
- Reduces Risk Of Cardiovascular Disease
- Preserves Lean Body Mass
- Increases Self-Esteem
- Decreases Hostility
- Improves Diet
- Reduces Intensity Of Stress Response
- Increases Quality Of Life
- Improves Mental Alertness
- Helps Manage Stress
- Increases Muscular Strength
- Burns Calories
- Improves Glucose Tolerance
- Reduces Risk Of Diabetes
- Reduces Sick Days
- Improves Athletic Performance
- Increases Stroke Volume
- Combats Substance Abuse
- Improves Oxygen Metabolism
- Improves Oxygen Intake
- Improves Oxygen Circulation
- Aids In Weight Loss
- Aids In Better Sleep
- Relief From Headaches
- Lowers Blood Pressure
- Helps Boost Creativity
- Lowers Resting Heart Rate
- Lowers Cholesterol Levels
- Alleviates Back Pain
- Improves Body Posture
- Relieves Constipation
- Improves Balance
- Improves Coordination
- Improves Flexibility
- Boosts Immune System
- Increases Muscular Endurance
- Prevents Infections-Colds
- Relieves Anxiety
- Helps Relieve Jet Lag
- Improves Mood
- Reduces Endometriosis
- Lower Health-Care Costs
- Reduces Triglycerides
- Enhances Sexual Desire, Performance, And Satisfaction

Using the list above and personal experience, list at least ten specific benifits that you receive from your regular exercise program. If you don't have a regular exercise program, write down at least ten specific benefits you would like to receive.

Using the list above and personal experience, how do exercise and stress management affect one another? Be specific.

Harcourt, Inc.

EXERCISE 13.2
• Reprogramming Your Self-Talk About Exercise

If you are struggling to start or continue exercising, this exercise might prove helpful. From the section on self-talk about exercise--or from your own mind--write down several statements that you think would be useful for you in getting started and sticking with an exercise program.

Self-talk Statement #1:

Self-talk Statement #2:

Self-talk Statement #3:

Self-talk Statement #4:

Self-talk Statement #5:

EXERCISE 13.3
• Nutrition "FUN" Quiz

Take the nutrition quiz below to assess your nutrition knowledge. Answers can be found on the next page.

		True	False
1.	A cup of cooked broccoli has more Vitamin C than one navel orange.		
2.	"Extra light" oils are lower in fat grams and calories.		
3.	The bulk of a person's daily diet should consist of complex carbohydrates (also known as starches).		
4.	Vegetable flavored pastas (spinach, tomato, carrot, or beet) are more nutrient dense than regular pasta.		
5.	Enriched flour should be the first ingredient listed on a bread label if you want to get the most nutrients per slice.		
6.	If you meticulously trim the fat from all meats and discard the poultry skin from poultry products, you will eliminate most of the cholesterol.		
7.	A new fat substitute, Olestra, that has been approved by the FDA and is being used in snack foods carries a warning label for loose stools and abdominal cramping.		
8.	Canned fruits and vegetables have less nutrients (vitamins and minerals) when compared to fresh fruits and vegetables.		
9.	Regular margarine contains fewer calories and less fat than butter.		
10.	A taco salad at Taco Bell has less calories and fat grams than two bean burritos.		

Using the Internet, find two fascinating nutrition facts. These two nutrition facts should be something that most people would not know. Be sure to cite the sources where your facts were found.

Fascinating Nutrition Fact #1:

Source #1:

Fascinating Nutrition Fact #2:

Source #2:

NUTRITION "FUN" QUIZ ANSWERS

1. **True** - One cup of broccoli has 98 mg of Vitamin C compared to one naval orange which has 80 mg. Three ounces of red bell pepper has the highest amount of Vitamin C at 163 mg, followed by three ounces of green bell pepper at 110 mg.

2. **False** - "Extra light" oils are lighter in flavor but not lower in fat grams or calories.

3. **True** - A person should center their diet around complex carbohydrates or starches, such as bread, pasta, potatoes, rice, and cereal.

4. **False** - Unfortunately the only difference between vegetable flavored pasta and regular pasta is the color. For example, it only takes a minute amount of spinach (approximately one tablespoon) to color an entire batch of pasta noodles.

5. **False** - The first ingredient listed should be whole wheat flour if you want to receive the most nutrients from the bread you eat.

6. **False** - Cholesterol is found inside the cells of meat products, therefore it cannot be removed. Removing the excess fat and skin from meat products will, however, lower the amount of fat and calories per serving.

7. **True** - Olestra is a new fat substitute from Proctor & Gamble which is synthesized from sugar and fatty acids. It passes through the body without being digested or absorbed, so it has no calories. Unfortunately, a large number of public health and nutrition experts believe olestra isn't a dream come true, but, in fact, a nightmare. Olestra has some side-effects which include abdominal cramping, loose stools, and depletion of fat-soluble vitamins. Despite these side-effects, the FDA approved the use of olestra in snack foods if the foods carry a warning label which reads: This product contains olestra. Olestra may cause abdominal cramping and loose stools. Olestra inhibits the absorption of some vitamins and other nutrients. Vitamins A, D, E, and K have been added.

8. **False** - Don't overlook canned and frozen vegetables and fruits. Thanks to improved technology, canned and frozen produce retains most of the food's vitamins and minerals. Commercially canned and frozen produce is usually processed immediately after picking and close to the field. "Fresh" vegetables and fruits are not necessarily more nutritious, since many are harvested before they're ripe, trucked thousands of miles, and stored for long periods--in which case nutrient losses can be great. Canned beans, pumpkin, corn, pineapple, spinach, and beets, to name a few, are actually quite nutritious. But watch out for one unwanted extra: lots of sodium.

9. **False** - Regular margarine and butter both contain about the same amount of fat and calories per teaspoon.

10. **False** - A taco salad from taco bell (without the ranch dressing) has 61 grams of fat and 905 calories. Each bean burrito has 14 grams of fat and 381 calories. Not eating the taco shell, can reduce the calories and fat grams almost in half (484 calories and 31 fat grams).

EXERCISE 13.4
• Fiber, Fruits, And Vegetables: Are You Getting Enough?

Diet can have a significant impact on the development, prevention, and treatment of diseases and illnesses. This exercise focuses on the impact of daily fiber, vegetable, and fruit intake on the development of cancer. Nutritionists agree that Americans should consume 20 to 30 grams of fiber a day and at least three servings of vegetables and two servings of fruits. For the next two days calculate your daily fiber, vegetable, and fruit intake.   Use the table below and food labels to calculate fiber grams. When counting vegetable and fruit servings, don't forget to include "hidden" vegetables found in marinara sauces, soups, and sandwiches.

Day One:

Total Servings of Fruit	Total Servings of Vegetables	Total Fiber Grams

Day Two:

Total Servings of Fruit	Total Servings of Vegetables	Total Fiber Grams

Food	Fiber Content
• High-fiber wheat-bran cereal (1 oz.) • Pinto, kidney, navy beans (dried, cooked, ½ C)	**More than 5 grams**
• Oat bran, oatmeal (dry, 1 oz.) • Barley (dry, 1 oz.) • Berries (1/2 C) • Apple, pear (medium, w/ skin) • Orange, grapefruit (medium) • Figs, prunes (dried, 3) • Okra, cabbage, peas, turnips, sweet potato (cooked, ½ C) • Carrots (cooked, ½ C) • Chick-peas, split peas, lima beans (cooked, ½ C)	**2 - 5 grams**
• Peach, nectarine (medium) • Apricots (2) • Whole wheat bread (1 slice) • Pasta (cooked, 1 C) • Rye bread (1 slice) • Corn (1/2 C) • Low-fiber wheat cereal (1 oz.) • Cauliflower (cooked, ½ C)	**1 - 2 grams**

Write a brief essay, describing what have you learned from this exercise. Consider the following questions:
• **Are you meeting the minimum requirements for fiber, fruits, and vegetables?**
• **How could you increase the amount of fiber, fruits, and vegetables in your daily diet?**

Harcourt, Inc.

EXERCISE 13.5

• Vitamin And Mineral Supplements: Cheap Investment Or Expensive Urine?

Based on the information on vitamins and other supplements in Chapter 13 and personal experience, write a brief essay explaining your view on supplements. Consider the following questions:

• **Are supplements used too much in our society?**

• **When do you think supplements are useful?**

• **Are supplements cheap insurance for good health in today's society?**

EXERCISE 13.6
• Evaluating Your Food Scripts

Your food script is part of your broader life script--a blueprint for living developed through early messages and early decisions. Answer the following questions to increase your awareness of the food scripts in your life.

1. **Recall some childhood experiences that involved food and eating. What messages (both positive and negative) did you receive about food and eating from family and friends?**

2. **Have these messages either contributed to your wellness or caused problems with your wellness?**

3. **What steps can you take to change the negative messages you received about food and eating from family and friends to minimize distress and maximize wellness?**

EXERCISE 13.7
• Stress And Eating Habits

There are a number of linkages between nutrition and stress. One common link is that stress often influences a person's eating habits. Some people overeat, some people don't eat enough, and some people crave specific foods in response to the stressors in their lives. For the next three days, keep a food diary using the table below: [The stress level is a subjective measure of arousal. Ask yourself on a scale from 0 to 10 (O representing no arousal and 10 representing total overload) how much arousal you feel both before and after eating.]

Time	Food	Activity & Feeling(s) Before Eating	Stress Level Before Eating	Activity & Feeling(s) After Eating	Stress Level After Eating

1. **What did you learn about your eating habits? Does the stress in your life influence your eating habits?**

2. **What changes would you like to make in your diet that would minimize the amount of distress you experience?**

Harcourt, Inc.

EXERCISE 13.8
• Eating Disorders And Stress

Considering the information in Chapter 13 and personal experience, write a brief essay explaining how stress and eating disorders are linked. Be sure to consider the sociological linkages, as well as physiological and psychological linkages.

EXERCISE 13.9
• Assessing And Improving Your Sleep Habits

Sleep is an essential health buffer that allows us to reach our full potential during the day. When we don't get enough sleep, we increase the likelihood of distress. Use the assessment below to take a closer look at how you might minimize distress by changing your current sleep habits.

1. **What are your main sleep problems, if any?**

	Often a Problem	Sometimes a Problem	Seldom a Problem
Difficulty Falling Asleep			
Difficulty Sleep Through the Night			
Too Little Sleep			
Too Much Sleep			
Irregular Sleep Habits			

2. **Steps I can take to improve my sleep habits include:**

Harcourt, Inc.

CHAPTER 13 SELF-TEST

Instructions: Circle true or false. Answers can be found in the appendix.

1. Researchers estimate that for every hour exercised, two hours of life expectancy are added.
   True   **False**

2. Schafer's aerobic exercise guidelines for purposes of effective stress control and high-level wellness include exercising at least 30 to 40 minutes, 5 - 7 days per week, at an intensity of 60 - 90 percent of estimated maximum heart rate.
   True   **False**

3. Sympathomimetic agents are foods that are eaten to draw sympathy from others.
   True   **False**

4. According to the Food Guide Pyramid, a person should consume approximately five servings from the bread, cereal, rice, and pasta group.
   True   **False**

5. HDL (high density lipoprotein) is the "bad guy" of cholesterol because it deposits cholesterol along the walls of the coronary arteries.
   True   **False**

6. In general, most people would benefit from vitamin supplements.
   True   **False**

7. Eating disorders, such as obesity, anorexia, and bulimia, are most often the direct result of intense stress.
   True   **False**

8. Studies have shown that eating three big meals a day is better than eating small meals throughout the day combined with several snacks.
   True   **False**

9. The deepest sleep a person experiences occurs during REM (rapid-eye-movement) sleep.
   True   **False**

10. Healthy pleasures can also be seen as personal anchors.
    True   **False**

Application Exercises for
CHAPTER 14:
Self-Talk, Beliefs, and Meaning

EXERCISE 14.1
• Monitoring Threatening Situations

We know that the demands in our lives do not cause distress. It is our interpretation of the demands that causes distress. Complete the following exercise during the next three days.

1. Identify specific circumstances in which you felt emotional or physical distress.

2. To what extent did you interpret the stressor to be a threat under each circumstance?

3. Was your interpretation realistic or faulty?

4. What alternative interpretations might you have used in each case?

Harcourt, Inc.

EXERCISE 14.2

• Your Favorite Styles Of Negative Situational Self-Talk And Realistic Alternatives

Consider the styles of negative self-talk that are discussed in Chapter 14 (Negativizing, Awfulizing, Catastrophizing, Overgeneralizing, Minimizing, Blaming, Perfectionism, Musterbation, Personalizing, Judging Human Worth, Control Fallacy, Polarized Thinking, Being Right, Fallacy of Fairness, Shoulding, and Magnifying) to complete this exercise.

In the left-hand column below, write down the four styles of negative self-talk that you currently use more often than you would like. In the right-hand column, write in helpful self-talk that will help eliminate each negative style.

Style of Negative Self-Talk	Realistic Self-Talk Alternative

Now, choose one positive self-talk statement you would most like to learn. Write the positive self-talk statement on a 3- by 5-inch card, and review your card many times each day. Apply it.

Harcourt, Inc.

EXERCISE 14.3
• Using The Situational Self-Talk Tools

The first step in changing any negative habit is awareness. The same rule applies to self-talk. A person must first become aware of the negative self-talk before it can be changed. The situational self-talk tools discussed in Chapter 14 (P and Q method, Instant Replay, and Realistic Self-talk) are extremely helpful for increasing awareness of negative self-talk. Use the table below to chart your use of these tools over the next several days.

Situation	Negative Self-Talk	Tool Used

EXERCISE 14.4
• Rewriting Irrational Beliefs

The first step in rewriting irrational beliefs is to recognize them in your own daily thinking. The next step is to question them. The third is to change them. Use the questions below to help you get started on rewriting your irrational beliefs. (A list of twenty common irrational beliefs can be found in Chapter 14).

1. **List the irrational beliefs you recognize as more present in yourself than you would like.**

2. **List three irrational beliefs that you would most like to change below. Below each irrational belief you want to change, write a more rational or reasonable version. Be sure to keep in mind the three criteria of rational beliefs: factual, moderate, and helpful.**

    Irrational Belief #1:

    Revised Belief #1:

    Irrational Belief #2:

    Revised Belief #2:

    Irrational Belief #3:

    Revised Belief #3:

3. **What concrete differences would it make in your life to act on these new reasonable beliefs?**

Harcourt, Inc.

EXERCISE 14.5
• Creating Vicious- And Vital-Cycle Scenarios

Knowing that vicious cycles are caused by negative beliefs and vital cycles are caused by positive beliefs, create hypothetical vicious- and vital-cycle scenarios, beginning with the beliefs listed below.

1. (a) I am at my best when challenged.

    (b) I am at my worst when challenged.

2. (a) Nobody ever likes me.

    (b) I am a reasonably likable person.

3. (a) Most people are out to take advantage of me.

    (b) Most people are motivated most of the time by good will.

4. (a) Outside events upset me.

    (b) I upset myself through my interpretation of events.

5. (a) I cannot change.

    (b) I can change, although it sometimes takes hard work and patience.

Harcourt, Inc.

EXERCISE 14.6
• Reprogramming Your Self-Talk

Old, irrational beliefs will continue to provide the basis for situational interpretations--and for harmful distress--unless they are changed. Reprogramming is a very powerful tool for changing a pattern of negative self-talk to a pattern of realistic or positive self-talk. Use the questions below to reprogram your self-talk.

1. **Identify a specific repetitive situation in which you respond emotionally or behaviorally in unwanted ways.**

2. **Identify the negative self-talk you use to upset yourself.**

3. **Create a new self-talk alternative for reprogramming your thinking (or take one from a list in this book). Be sure the new statement meets the five criteria--personal, positive, present-tense, practical, and brief.**

4. **Write this statement on a 3- by 5-inch card. Carry this card with you, or put it in a conspicuous place where you will see it many times each day. Repeat it over and over-- perhaps 30 times per day. After two or three weeks, you will find the new statement a natural part of your thinking, influencing your emotions and behavior quite differently from the old self-talk.**

Harcourt, Inc.

EXERCISE 14.7
• Just Stick It!

This exercise works in cooperation with the other self-talk tools to help reinforce the use of positive self-talk statements. To complete this exercise you will need a couple of self-adhesive post-it notes.

1. **Write down a specific situation in which you frequently experience distress. The situation might involve work, driving or parking, body image, exercise, nutrition or sleep habits, relationships, or school.**

2. **Write a positive self-talk statement on several post-it notes that is specific for the situation identified above.**

3. **Now, you want to stick the post-it notes where you will see them several times a day. For example, if you experience a lot of distress when driving, put several post-it notes in your car to help remind you to use the new self-talk statements when you need them most.**

Harcourt, Inc.

EXERCISE 14.8
• Perfectionism And Achievement

One might ask, is not internal perfectionism vital for personal, academic, and professional success? Doesn't setting exceedingly high standards motivate one to strive higher? It is our position that perfectionism is counterproductive, rather than helpful for success. Consider the contrasting philosophies of achievement described below.

Perfectionism View of Achievement	Wellness View of Achievement
• I *must* do it perfectly.	• I will strive to do my best.
• If I do not do it perfectly, I deserve to *punish* myself.	• I will accept what I have done--for now.
• Since I *did not* do it perfectly, I certainly *must* do it perfectly in the future	• I will learn from that effort to seek to improve next time.

1. What do you think are the results of each philosophy?

2. Which philosophy most closely fits your current outlook?

3. Which philosophy will you strive toward in the future?

Harcourt, Inc.

EXERCISE 14.9
• Reprogramming To Reduce Worrying

As described in Chapter 14, there are several practical applications for reprogramming one's self-talk. This exercise specifically looks at reducing worrying (a distress-prone personality pattern discussed in Chapter 9).

From the section in this chapter on worry--or from your own mind--write below several self-talk statements you think would be useful for reducing your own worry tendencies.

Write one of these on a 3- by 5-inch card, carry the card with you or put it in a visible place, and repeat this statement, 10, 20, or 30 times a day. You will find the statement becoming part of your normal thinking.

Harcourt, Inc.

EXERCISE 14.10
• Reprogramming To Strengthen Hardiness

In addition to using reprogramming to minimize negative qualities, one can use reprogramming to maximize positive qualities. This exercise specifically looks at strengthening the 3 C's of hardiness (challenge, commitment, and control) described in Chapter 10.

From the section in this chapter on hardiness--or from your own mind--write below several self-talk statements you think would be useful for strengthening your own hardiness.

Write one of these on a 3- by 5-inch card, carry the card with you or put it in a visible place, and repeat this statement, 10, 20, or 30 times a day. You will find the statement becoming part of your normal thinking.

Harcourt, Inc.

EXERCISE 14.11
• Discovering Negative Self-Talk About Self-Esteem

Self-esteem (self-liking or self-acceptance) is the result of positive self-talk about the self. As discussed in Chapter 10, self-esteem is a key personal quality adding to distress-resistance--as well as to chances of success, good health, and positive relationships. Answer the questions below to discover any negative self-talk that you might use concerning your self-esteem.

1. Think of a recent compliment. What was your verbal response to it?

2. What criticism have you faced? What was your internal and external reply?

3. List a project or activity you have begun or considered beginning. What did you tell yourself as you started or failed to start it?

4. What beliefs about yourself have you shared in intimate conversation with another? Were these beliefs negative or positive?

5. Think of a situation (time, place, surroundings) where you tend to feel negative about yourself. What do you typically say to yourself while in this situation?

6. Consider a time when you generally feel positive about yourself.

7. Do you have a common physical symptom? What is your symptom telling you?

8. Do you find yourself engaging in "wistful thinking?" Do you often procrastinate? If so, from what negative self-talk are you escaping?

Source: Butler (1981, 79). Reprinted with permission.

Harcourt, Inc.

EXERCISE 14.12
• Using Self-Talk To Build Self-Esteem

Self-esteem (self-liking or self-acceptance) is the result of positive self-talk about the self. As discussed in Chapter 10, self-esteem is a key personal quality adding to distress-resistance--as well as to chances of success, good health, and positive relationships. Use this exercise to increase your self-esteem through the use of new positive self-talk statements about yourself.

1.   From the section in this chapter on self-esteem--or from your own mind--write below several self-talk statements you think would be useful for strengthening your own self-esteem.

2.   Write one of these on a 3- by 5-inch card, carry the card with you or put it in a visible place, and repeat this statement, 10, 20, or 30 times a day. You will find the statement becoming part of your normal thinking.

3.   What benefits could you expect to receive from using these new self-talk statements? Consider all aspects of your wellness.

Harcourt, Inc.

EXERCISE 14.13
• The Ardell M & P In Life Review

Please circle the following statement choices about meaning and purpose (M & P) as true or false. Tell the truth, be honest, and keep your eyes straight ahead--no cheating!

My daily life is, for the most part, interesting, pleasurable, and meaningful, and my commitments and values extend beyond my own immediate concerns.	True	False
If asked, I can describe how I find meaning and purpose, and I'm not hesitant or shy about doing so.	True	False
I enjoy all or most of the people with whom I associate, even those who are essentially creeps, blowhards, and misfits.	True	False
I would not make drastic changes if I knew I had just months to live. I may not hang around this dump, but I would still be the same kind of person.	True	False
I'm confident that my existence has had a net positive effect on a number of other people.	True	False
To prepare for this question, consider the scene in the movie *Forrest Gump* (even if you have not seen it), when the lead character reflects on the meaning of life while standing at his young wife's grave. Gump thinks of all that has happened and wonders, "Do we have a destiny to fulfill, or are we just floating around on a breeze?", somewhat life the feather in the opening and closing scenes of the movie. The question, then, is this: Would you agree that, fulfilling a destiny, floating on a breeze, or something else, you can deal with it?	True	False
My work/career/profession contributes to a sense of meaning and purpose, or at least I have enough opportunities to indulge these feelings from my avocational pursuits.	True	False
I can't think of any goals or desires that I've long wanted to do but have not, out of fear or other reasons.	True	False
I spend most of my days doing what I think is necessary, appropriate, and reasonable; I don't feel constrained or stuck doing what others define as "shoulds" that contradict or offend my sense of what's right.	True	False
I am comfortable with questions about meaning and purpose; I don't feel a need to defend certainties or sacred truths.	True	False

Whether you answered true or false on these questions, ask yourself what your holy grail looks like and where the search for it might take you.

Source: Ardell Wellness Report (Fall 1994, 4). Used by permission. For further information on the Ardell Wellness Report, write Donald B. Ardell, 345 Bayshore Blvd. #414, Tampa, FL 33606.

Harcourt, Inc.

CHAPTER 14 SELF-TEST

Instructions: Circle true or false. Answers can be found in the appendix.

1. Your interpretation of stressors, not stressors themselves, causes distress.
   True   **False**

2. Self-talk influences one's emotions, mental pictures, physical states, and behavior.
   True   **False**

3. The self-talk statement "I know he is upset because of what I said to him earlier" is an example of negativizing.
   True   **False**

4. In the P & Q method, the P stands for please and the Q stands for quiet.
   True   **False**

5. The three C's of Instant Replay used for managing situational self-talk are challenge it, change it, and control it.
   True   **False**

6. Disputation involves challenging other people's viewpoints.
   True   **False**

7. The vicious cycle is caused by bound energy.
   True   **False**

8. For new self-talk messages to be effective, they should be in the future tense.
   True   **False**

9. Two practical applications of reprogramming self-talk are reducing hostility and increasing self-esteem.
   True   **False**

10. All anger is a negative part of human experience and should be avoided.
    True   **False**

Application Exercises for CHAPTER 15: Relaxation Methods

EXERCISE 15.1
• Using The Mental Rehearsal Method

Using the mental rehearsal method can be very helpful in maximizing performance under challenging conditions, whether it be an upcoming test, paper, athletic event, public speech, job interview, date or a difficult encounter with an adversary or partner. Use the mental rehearsal method sometime during the next week. Use the questions below to describe your experience.

1. What was the specific event in which you used mental rehearsal?

2. Briefly describe the mental rehearsal you created.

3. How did mental rehearsal help you during the specific situation?

EXERCISE 15.2
• Dispelling The Myths Of Hypnosis

Hypnosis is a very old and effective method of producing deep relaxation, but some people associate hypnosis with a carnival side show where hypnotized people are clucking like chickens and taking off their clothes. Hypnosis is gradually becoming more accepted by a more enlightened society and clinical/medical communities, but there are still several myths associated with hypnosis. Answer the questions below to dispel the common myths that are often associated with hypnosis. Be sure to cite your sources where your information was obtained.

1. **Briefly define hypnotherapy.**

2. **What are the different types of hypnotherapists? What are the requirements for certification?**

3. **How is hypnotherapy being used within the clinical/medical community? Give specific examples.**

4. **List at least five specific examples of how hypnosis can be used to increase one's wellness.**

5. **After your research, would you consider being hypnotized? How could you personally benefit from hypnotherapy?**

Harcourt, Inc.

EXERCISE 15.3
• Search For Scientific Evidence

There are an incredible number of different relaxation methods people can choose from. Some of these methods have been around for centuries and some are a result of the latest craze. Using the Internet, do one search on a relaxation technique described in Chapter 15 and one search on a new relaxation technique that isn't mentioned in the text. Use the following exercise to report what you found.

1. **The relaxation technique described in Chapter 15 that I chose to search was:**

   My source was:

   Briefly summarize the article you found.

   Did the information in your article affect your personal view of this relaxation technique? Explain.

2. **A new relaxation technique that I found was:**

   My source was:

   Briefly summarize the article you found.

   What conclusion can you reasonably draw about the scientific support--or lack of it--for this relaxation technique? Are future studies needed?

   From the information you obtained, would you be willing to try this new relaxation technique? Explain.

EXERCISE 15.4
• Effects Of Music On Arousal And Relaxation

As an "experiment-of-one," try the following to increase your awareness of the effects of different kinds of music on your physical and mental arousal and relaxation. Use the table below to chart your experiment.

1. **Listen to a different type of music at the same time and under the same conditions each day for several days. This might be during your deep relaxation time, while washing dishes, studying, doing housework, or whenever. Each day, select quite different types of music: country and western, new age, easy classical, dramatic classical, big band, hard rock, romantic vocal, or whatever.**

2. **Listen for at least ten minutes. At the end of that time, write down your reactions as follows:**
   • **Your tension level and mood before starting**
   • **What you experienced in mind and body while listening.**
   • **What you experienced in mind and body during the subsequent hour**

Type of Music	Condition	Tension Level and Mood (before starting)	What I Experienced in Mind & Body (while listening)	What I Experienced in Mind & Body (during subsequent hour)

What did you learn from this experiment about the effects of music on arousal and relaxation?

EXERCISE 15.5
• Locating Relaxation Resources In Your Area

Learning more about the relaxation resources in your community can help you maximize the variety of relaxation methods you use on a daily basis. Find a combination of five resources in your area that focus on relaxation techniques. (These resources could be classes, expert instruction, facilities, or services.) If available, learn about the following with each: where, when, how often, cost, qualifications of instructor, and claims of advertisements. Use the table below to record your findings.

Name of Class, Expert Instruction, or other Resource	Where	When	How Often	Cost	Qualifications	Claims of Ads

Harcourt, Inc.

EXERCISE 15.6
• Experimenting With Daily Relaxation

The real challenge of daily relaxation is making it part of your daily routine with regularity and consistency. Try at least four different deep relaxation exercises discussed in Chapter 15 during the next week. Use the table below to record your experiences.

Type of Deep Relaxation	How I Felt During the Exercise	How I Felt After the Exercise

Based on your experiences, write a brief essay considering the following questions:
• **Which deep relaxation exercises will you use again in the future?**
• **Would you modify any of the exercises?**
• **What personal benefits could you receive by making deep relaxation part of your daily routine?**

CHAPTER 15 SELF-TEST

Instructions: Circle true or false. Answers can be found in the appendix.

1. The relaxation response is controlled through the sympathetic and parasympathetic nervous systems.
    True   **False**

2. Aerobic exercise is a hypometabolic approach to stress control.
    True   **False**

3. Breathing exercises are effective because when your lungs slow down, you will feel a calming effect throughout your body.
    True   **False**

4. Meditation and contemplation are synonymous terms.
    True   **False**

5. Zen meditation differs from the other techniques in that one allows the mind to wander and drift.
    True   **False**

6. Visualization is a technique commonly used for deep relaxation.
    True   **False**

7. The point of self-hypnosis is to induce deep quiet through self-suggestion, much like mediation or autogenic relaxation.
    True   **False**

8. EKG, EEG, and GSR are all examples of biofeedback relaxation techniques that have been developed to make invisible internal processes visible.
    True   **False**

9. Progressive muscle relaxation is practiced by focusing self-suggestions of warmth and heaviness in specific muscle groups throughout the body.
    True   **False**

10. Hydrotherapy can be a very effective method of relaxation.
    True   **False**

Harcourt, Inc.

Application Exercises for CHAPTER 16: Managing Time

EXERCISE 16.1
• It's As Easy As ABC!

The first step in managing time more effectively is to be clear what is urgent to get done, what is rather important, and what can wait. The exercise below will help prioritize your tasks for the upcoming week by using the ABC-technique, as described in Chapter 16.

1. **Use the space below to write down everything you need to accomplish during the upcoming week. Don't forget to write down personal tasks, such as exercising, spending time with friends, or relaxing.**

2. **Use the table below to prioritize all of the tasks you listed.**

My priorities for the week of: _____

A Tasks (Must Do!)	B Tasks (Should Do)	C Tasks (Nice to Do)

EXERCISE 16.2
• Making Lists Work For You

To-do lists can be very helpful. Some people make one to-do list at the beginning of the week, adding to it when needed. Others make a daily to-do list, compiling their list first thing in the morning or the night before. Either way, to-do lists save time and decrease distress. When compiling your to-do list, avoid creating unrealistically long lists or setting unrealistic deadlines. Remember most to-do lists are not written in stone, so give yourself credit for chipping away at your list even if all your tasks haven't been completed. You may have your own system for creating a to-do list. If it works, keep it, if not try the following:

My To-Do List for: _____

Calls or E-mail	Shopping	Assignments (Reading or Homework)	Household	Work	Personal

Harcourt, Inc.

EXERCISE 16.3
• Taking Steps To Prevent Procrastination

From the information on procrastination we covered in Chapter 9, we know procrastination means to put something off you know you need to do or want to do and that procrastination is usually the result of self-talk. Drawing on the ten techniques for overcoming procrastination, write a brief essay completing the sentence below.

10 Techniques for Overcoming Procrastination
(See Chapter 16 for a brief description of each technique.)

"Knockout Technique"	Five-Minute Plan
Small Sequential Steps	Self-Reward
"Swiss Cheese" Method	Self-Punishment
"Work First Approach"	Cost-Benefit Analysis
"Remember Forgetting" Technique	Stimulus Control

In order to prevent or reduce procrastination, I will:

Harcourt, Inc.

EXERCISE 16.4
• Time vs. Money

If you asked people ten years ago which is the most precious commodity (money or time), most of them would have answered money. But according to the latest polls, the majority of people report that time is the most precious commodity. It is suggested that money can always be made, but once a minute has passed there is no way to get it back. One good example of how time is viewed as more precious than money is the fact that a lot of people spend money to save time. Use the space below to write a brief essay answering the following question:

Is time or money your most precious commodity?

EXERCISE 16.5
• Identifying Your Risk Factors For Boredom

Stress can become a problem on either end of the continuum: overload or underload. For some people, the problem is underload, or boredom. Use the following assessment to see if you are experiencing boredom.

	Very True	Somewhat True	Not Very True
Insufficient Challenge			
Too Much Isolation			
Too Much Routine			
Meaninglessness			

1. What steps can you take, based on personal responsibility, for minimizing such experiences in the future?

2. Remember that experiences are never boring of themselves: they become boring only when they are interpreted that way. What self-talk might you use to turn boredom into a positive experience?

EXERCISE 16.6
• Applying The Miscellaneous Time-Management Tips
Schafer lists a number of specific time-management tips at the end of Chapter 16. Use this exercise to see which tips you could use to better manage your time and decrease the amount of distress in your daily life.

1. Put a checkmark next to the miscellaneous time-management tips you could benefit from using.

2. List below the three tips that would bring you the most benefits.

3. When will you begin using each one of these tips listed above? Be specific.

EXERCISE 16.7
• Examining Irrational Beliefs About Time

A key step for reducing chronic time urgency is to reexamine your beliefs or assumptions about time--and where needed, to alter those beliefs that are irrational or unreasonable. Use the assessment below to see which of the eleven common irrational beliefs about time apply to you.

	Applies A GREAT DEAL to me	Applies QUITE A BIT to me	Applies SOMEWHAT to me	Applies VERY LITTLE to me	Applies NOT AT ALL to me
I must always be productive.					
What matters most in life is getting ahead, being productive, or winning competitive struggles.					
I cannot delegate because no one can meet my standards.					
I will be able to enjoy myself only after catching up with all I have to do.					
I must always get the most possible done in the least possible time.					
I must usually hurry to get everything done.					
If I spend time relaxing, resting, or exercising, I will certainly fall behind in more important things.					
I cannot help but be upset or anxious when a task is incomplete.					
I have no control over constant overload in my life.					
There is no way I can be happy if I'm overloaded. I can't stand it.					
I must be all things to all people.					

1. **Rewrite those irrational beliefs that you noted as applying somewhat, quite a lot, or a great deal to you, making them positive, rational beliefs about time.**

2. **How would your life be different if you were to genuinely accept and act on these alternative beliefs?**

3. **What step will you take first to act on one of these beliefs?**

Harcourt, Inc.

EXERCISE 16.8
• Avoiding Time Bandits

Time bandits are basically tasks, people, or things in our lives that rob us of time. Most people feel more pressed for time than ever before. But according to the latest findings, we actually may have more time than we think. Researchers estimate that we have more leisure time than thirty years ago. So why doesn't it feel that way? The answer may be found in evaluating your time bandits. Two of the biggest time bandits are recreational shopping and watching television. Shopping has become more time consuming, not to mention more stressful, because of the increase in consumer products. Watching television has become a popular way to relax, even though television doesn't offer the kind of psychological release from stress we need in today's fast paced society. It isn't coincidental that a lot of our free time comes in short spurts that seem to be tailor-made for watching thirty minute television shows. Answer the following questions to identify and reduce your time bandits.

1. **List your top five time bandits. If you aren't sure where your time goes, consider keeping track of what you're doing during your day, especially during leisure hours.**

2. **Why do you think recreational shopping and watching television have been identified as the two biggest time bandits in our society? Be specific.**

3. **When you have fifteen minutes or more to spare, instead of turning on the television, what else could you do to receive more pleasure out of your leisure time?**

EXERCISE 16.9
• How Organized Are You?

To assess how organized you are, complete the following assessment. Answer each question with either "yes" or "no."

	Yes	No
Are you almost always late to classes, meetings and appointments?		
Do you find yourself always making apologies for being disorganized?		
Do you plan only a day at a time--never weeks or months in advance?		
Do you find that you "don't have time" for those essential activities that help you take care of yourself--exercise, relaxation, preparing and eating good food, music and arts, and quality time with family and friends?		
At the end of a day, do you often feel that you've been dealing with trivia and haven't done the more important things?		
Do you feel you'd like to be more organized, but your life is such a mess you wouldn't know where to begin?		
Is your refrigerator badly in need of cleaning?		
Do you often forget or misplace your keys, glasses, handbag, briefcase, appointment book, and the like?		
Do you find yourself constantly running out of essential supplies at home or at work?		
Have you forgotten a scheduled appointment within the past month?		

Scoring: Give yourself one point for every "yes" answer.

0 - 1 point	Congratulations! You have things pretty well under control!
2 - 4 points	Somewhat disorganized.
5 - 7 points	Fairly disorganized. Following the time management guidelines in this chapter should be helpful.
8 - 10 points	Highly disorganized. Life is probably pretty difficult. The time management guidelines in this chapter could change your life!

Source: Medical Self-Care, 16 (Spring, 1982), 26

CHAPTER 16 SELF-TEST

Instructions: Circle true or false. Answers can be found in the appendix.

1. Our concept of time is culturally influenced.
   True   **False**

2. Researchers have found "feeling rushed" increases the likelihood of distress symptoms.
   True   **False**

3. The experience of social roles, obligations, and commitments that are easy to get into and difficult to get out of is called overload.
   True   **False**

4. The three categories of time-management principles and techniques are identifying, prioritizing, and scheduling.
   True   **False**

5. The ABC technique is a method of scheduling tasks.
   True   **False**

6. Time mapping involves blocking out several hours on a given day for a specific activity.
   True   **False**

7. Procrastinators have difficulty with implementing.
   True   **False**

8. Insufficient challenge and too much routine are two key risk factors for boredom.
   True   **False**

9. Chronic time urgency is the direct result of external pressures.
   True   **False**

10. Making time for healthy pleasures is a good time management tip.
    True   **False**

Harcourt, Inc.

Application Exercises for
CHAPTER 17:
Social Support

EXERCISE 17.1
• Social-Support Scale

Complete the brief survey below about the social support in your life. Circle the number that best describes your answer for the questions below.

	Agree	Uncertain	Disagree
I usually feel pretty lonely.	1	2	3
When times are tough for me, there is no one available to provide genuine "moral support."	1	2	3
I have close friends to provide me plenty of emotional support when I need it.	3	2	1
Generally speaking, I have a pretty good sense of belonging or connectedness to those around me.	3	2	1

Total your score for all four questions (Score = _____). See Exercise 17.2 to compare and assess your score.

Harcourt, Inc.

EXERCISE 17.2
• Comparing and Assessing Your Social-Support Scale

Below are the percentages of 276 undergraduate students who gave each response to items in the Social Support Scale, as well as the distribution of their total scores.

	Agree	Uncertain	Disagree
I usually feel pretty lonely.	18%	22%	60%
When times are tough for me, there is no one available to provide genuine "moral support."	7%	8%	85%
I have close friends to provide me plenty of emotional support when I need it.	73%	13%	13%
Generally speaking, I have a pretty good sense of belonging or connectedness to those around me.	73%	14%	13%

Distribution of total scores of 276 undergraduate students:

	SCORE	PERCENT OF RESPONDENTS
HIGH SOCIAL SUPPORT	12	43%
MEDIUM SOCIAL SUPPORT	10 - 11	31%
LOW SOCIAL SUPPORT	4 - 9	25%

On a separate sheet of paper, write a brief essay describing what you learned from your responses to each question and from your total score.

EXERCISE 17.3
• Assessing And Applying Communication Guidelines

Use this exercise to become more aware of how often you currently practice each of the eight communication guidelines listed below.

	Most of the time	Sometimes	Seldom
I own my feelings and thoughts.			
I address the other person directly.			
I make statements rather than ask questions.			
I don't sandbag my negative feelings.			
When giving feedback, I describe the effects of the other's actions rather than be accusatory.			
I am generous in giving positive feedback to others.			
I practice active listening.			
I speak only for myself and not for others.			

The guidelines I would most like to apply more in my life are:

Specific steps I will take to apply these include:

Harcourt, Inc.

EXERCISE 17.4
• Assessing Your Self-Disclosure Habits

Self-disclosure is the process of revealing authentic, personal thoughts and feelings to others. Self-disclosure entails risk, but usually the risk is worth taking because self-disclosure often leads to building satisfying relationships. Complete the following assessment on self-disclosure. There are no right or wrong answers or scoring standards for this assessment. Rather, these questions are intended simply to help you become more aware of your self-disclosure habits.

Put a checkmark next to the following statements with which you agree.

_____ 1. **I seldom share my true feelings with anyone.**

_____ 2. **Those with whom I work (or go to school) know little about what I'm thinking most of the time.**

_____ 3. **I usually feel better after expressing myself to someone I'm close to.**

_____ 4. **I wish I could get closer to others.**

_____ 5. **I wish I could open up more to others.**

_____ 6. **I would like to be more open to others and their feelings.**

_____ 7. **Being open with others usually ends up hurting me.**

_____ 8. **Others see me as quite honest and open.**

_____ 9. **My physical tension usually mounts when I hold in my feelings for very long.**

_____ 10. **My sleep is often disturbed by unexpressed feelings (either good or bad).**

Write a brief essay considering the following questions:
- **How satisfied are you with your answers?**
- **What can you learn from this assessment?**
- **What might you do differently in regards to your self-disclosure habits?**

Harcourt, Inc.

EXERCISE 17.5
• Practice Appropriate Active Listening Responses

Active listening is a simple skill that can do wonders for improving communication between two or more people. Active listeners should avoid using negative styles of communication (e.g., ordering, discounting, judging, psychologizing, defending, and parroting). To complete this exercise, write an appropriate active listening response for the following statements.

Sender: "I don't have time for this nonsense."
Listener: "You sure as heck do. Do it." (Ordering)
Active Listener:

Sender: "Why doesn't anyone ever take me seriously around here?"
Listener: "Poor John, no one ever listens to you." (Discounting)
Active Listener:

Sender: "Nothing ever works around here."
Listener: "Oh, come on, you are just tired and hot tonight." (Psychologizing)
Active Listener:

Sender: "I don't have time for this nonsense."
Listener: "What business do you have talking like that?" (Judging)
Active Listener:

Sender: "I'm so angry, I could scream."
Listener: "What do you mean? I did the best I could." (Defending)
Active Listener:

Sender: "I'm convinced I'm going to keep everything to myself from no on. You can't trust anyone around here."
Listener: "You sound like you can't trust anyone around here." (Parroting)
Active Listener:

Harcourt, Inc.

EXERCISE 17.6
• Communication Killers vs. Communication Enhancers

Monitor your own communication habits for the next couple of days. Using the information in Chapter 17 and the box below, answer the following questions about your communication habits.

Communication Killers	Communication Enhancers
Using threats • "If you do that, this relationship is over." **Criticizing** • "You really look stupid when you do that." **Blaming** • "It's all your fault." **Shoulding/Oughting** • "You should have done it this way." **Generalizing** (always or never) • "It's always the same thing with you." **Giving untimely advice** • "I told you so." **Interrupting** **Changing the topic** **Overusing why questions** **Beginning sentences with "You"**	**Being an active listener** • Maintaining eye contact • Asking for clarification • Rephrasing what you've heard • Focusing attention on the person • Really listening, not just waiting for your turn to speak **Using nonverbal messages** **Beginning sentences with "I"** **Being empathetic** **Using congruency** **Focusing on the present** **Avoid giving advice** (unless asked for) **Avoid diverting conversation to yourself**

1. Which communication enhancers do you regularly use?

2. Which communication killers do you use more often than you would like?

3. What steps will you take to become a better communicator in the future?

Harcourt, Inc.

EXERCISE 17.7
• Giving And Getting Criticism

Among the most volatile interchanges between one person and another is giving and receiving negative feedback. Distress can be minimized during the exchange of negative feedback when using guidelines that will help you focus objectively on the message being sent or received to remedy the situation through effective individual or joint problem-solving. Apply some of the guidelines described in Chapter 17 on giving and/or getting negative feedback. Use the following exercise to assess and improve your habits of giving and getting criticism.

1. **Did you exchange and accomplish what you had hoped? Explain.**

2. **What were the consequences for you? For the other person? For others in the environment? Distinguish between immediate and long-term effects.**

3. **What did you learn about yourself?**

4. **What might you do or say differently next time?**

Harcourt, Inc.

EXERCISE 17.8
• Trying Out Assertiveness

Assertiveness is a useful approach to coping effectively with the stressors in our lives. Assertiveness is desirable behavior for reducing tension in situations where there is potential buildup of resentment or anger, or when strength must be used to get what you want or to prevent someone else from imposing on you unnecessarily. Deliberately use some of the assertive self-talk and actions described in Chapter 17 in a real-life situation where it is timely and appropriate. Answer the following questions to assess your experience.

1. What was your self-talk before, during, and after the situation?

2. What did you feel?

3. How successful were you in accomplishing your objective? Explain.

4. What were the consequences for you? Your partner? Others?

5. What might you do differently next time?

Harcourt, Inc.

CHAPTER 17 SELF-TEST

Instructions: Circle true or false. Answers can be found in the appendix.

1. Social support refers to the specific set of linkages among a defined set of persons or a given person.
    True   **False**

2. The most important way true social support takes place in groups is through direct participation in central activities.
    True   **False**

3. Sam recently lost his wife of 25 years. His family and friends have provided significant support during this period and, as a result, he did not get sick once. This illustrates the direct effect of social support.
    True   **False**

4. Marriage has been shown to play an especially protective role against distress.
    True   **False**

5. A key to good communication is congruence within yourself.
    True   **False**

6. A person who too quickly and too completely reveals himself is known as a flasher.
    True   **False**

7. A consistent research finding is that self-disclosure begets self-disclosure.
    True   **False**

8. The three do's of active listening include being and appearing attentive, asking follow-up questions, and rephrasing what you have heard.
    True   **False**

9. Aggressiveness is desirable behavior for reducing tension in situations where there is potential buildup of resentment or anger.
    True   **False**

10. Positive strokes prevent and reduce distress for others and, through a loop-back effect, for the self.
    True   **False**

Harcourt, Inc.

Application Exercises for CHAPTER 18: Personal Wellness and Social Commitment

EXERCISE 18.1
• Altruistic Egoism And Egoistic Altruism

Altruistic egoism is Hans Selye's term for doing things others will appreciate and for which they will return their gratitude. Basically, altruistic egoism is earning others' love. Egoistic Altruism refers to self-fulfillment through contributing to the well-being of others. Answer the questions below to better understand these two concepts.

1. Give two specific examples of altruistic egoism and egoistic altruism.

   Altruistic Egoism Example #1:   Example #2:

   Egoistic Altruism Example #1:   Example #2:

2. Which of these two ideas do you find more appealing as a guideline in your own life? Why?

3. Which of these two ideas do you believe would be more advantageous to the entire society? Why?

Harcourt, Inc.

EXERCISE 18.2
• Random Acts Of Kindness

A random act of kindness includes doing something for another person (or group of people) without expecting anything in return. Some examples include: paying the bridge toll for the person behind you, sending flowers to someone anonymously, letting someone go in front of you in line, or thanking a manager for having such a great employee. Random acts of kindness are great examples of egoistic altruism. Often the best random acts of kindness are, in fact, random and done anonymously. Write a brief essay on the topic of random acts of kindness. Consider one or two of the following:

- **Describe the most memorable random act of kindness you did for someone.**
- **Describe the most memorable random act of kindness that was done for you.**
- **Describe some random acts of kindness you would like to do.**
- **What are some great examples of random acts of kindness you've heard from others or read about?**
- **Describe how you feel when you perform a random act of kindness?**
- **Describe how you feel when you've received a random act of kindness?**

Harcourt, Inc.

EXERCISE 18.3
• Your Personal Barriers To Social Responsibility

Negative self-talk is commonly used to prevent assumption of social responsibility for public problems. Answer the following questions to examine your own personal barriers to social responsibility.

1. Put a checkmark next to the self-talk barriers listed below in which you find yourself sometimes using as a justification for noninvolvement in other people's well-being or in civic matters? Explain.

    _____ I'll seem "goody-goody."
    _____ I'll seem holier than thou.
    _____ My motives will be suspect.
    _____ It's not my responsibility.
    _____ I don't know what to do.
    _____ I may make things worse.
    _____ I may look stupid.
    _____ Nothing I could do would make a difference.

2. Rewrite each of these self-talk statements so that they promote rather than impede social responsibility.

3. What differences would occur in the world if more people used these alternative self-talk statements?

Harcourt, Inc.

EXERCISE 18.4
• Environmental Wellness In Your Own Life

An integral part of one's wellness is their environment, both social and physical. One's personal wellness cannot flourish in a polluted natural environment. Wellness isn't an individual thing. Wellness means caring about the earth, as well as your own mind and body. Answer the following questions to focus on your environmental wellness.

1. **What actions do you now consciously take in your daily life to benefit the environment?**

2. **What actions might you begin taking to express your environmental wellness? When will you start? Be specific.**

EXERCISE 18.5
• Quality Living

Write a brief essay describing what quality of life means for you. For one person's statement, expressed as a poem, read the box, "Quality Living" in Chapter 18.

EXERCISE 18.6
• Is Your Body A Second-Class Citizen?

Sometimes in our fast paced society, we get so busy we treat our bodies as second-class citizens. Some people treat their material possessions better than their physical body. Answer the questions below to express your views on this subject.

1. Give specific examples of how Americans treat their bodies as second-class citizens.

2. What are some ways in which you treat your body as a second-class citizen?

3. What changes can you make to ensure that your body is treated as a first-class citizen?

EXERCISE 18.7
• Your Prescription For Stress Management

If you were writing a prescription for stress management, how would your prescription read.
Complete the following statement:

My prescription for stress management is......

CHAPTER 18 SELF-TEST

Instructions: Circle true or false. Answers can be found in the appendix.

1. Meaningful stress management and true wellness must include blending personal wellness with social commitment.
    True   **False**

2. Constructive maladjustment refers to people who are adjusting their negative habits constructively.
    True   **False**

3. Self-transcendence refers to the tendency of people to transfer their own problems onto others.
    True   **False**

4. Selye's term, altruistic egoism, means "to earn thy neighbor's love".
    True   **False**

5. Performing a *Random Act of Kindness* demonstrates the concept of egoistic altruism.
    True   **False**

6. Helping through a group effort has been found to relate more strongly to positive health outcomes than helping through an individual effort.
    True   **False**

7. Helping family or friends has been found to be more strongly associated with good health than helping strangers.
    True   **False**

8. The core of heroism is social responsibility.
    True   **False**

9. A person only experiences social barriers in the assumption of social responsibility.
    True   **False**

10. Cultural inhibition refers to the difficulty in adapting our way of life to technological change.
    True   **False**

APPENDIX

SELF-TEST ANSWERS

CHAPTER 1

1. True.
2. False - Experts estimate that between 50 - 80% of illnesses and diseases are stress-related.
3. False - The common cold and cancer are examples of how stress can cause an illness or disease by imposing long term wear and tear on the body and mind.
4. True.
5. False - Distress, even though by definition is harmful, can have positive effects.
6. False - The cost of distress affects family members, friends, co-workers, and anyone else who comes in contact with the person experiencing distress.
7. True.
8. False - A person's stress cannot be effectively managed without considering the social environment.
9. False - Egoistic altruism is the self-fulfillment one feels through promoting the well-being of others.
10. False - Constructive maladjustment refers to being appropriately concerned about social conditions and being motivated to do something about them.

CHAPTER 2

1. True.
2. False - It appears to be the accumulation of small daily hassles rather than acute (intense, yet short in duration) stressors, losing a loved one or a car accident, that wear an individual down mentally and physically.
3. False - People with an external locus of control feel their lifestyle choices have no influence on their life. They believe life is controlled by fate, destiny, chance, and luck.
4. True.
5. True.
6. False - Not only does inadequate preparation result in poor performance on tests, it does produce test anxiety.
7. False - This is an example of role strain because the student's personal desires are conflicting with others' expectations.
8. False - This is an example of role conflict. Specifically, Sandra is experiencing a conflict between two different roles (her role as an employee and her role as a student).
9. True.
10. False - Life scripts most often have a negative effect on one's wellness because they limit one's ability to respond authentically and spontaneously to a given situation.

Harcourt, Inc.

CHAPTER 3

1. True.
2. False - Being a critical thinker and open to new ideas may be affected by the emotional dimension of wellness, but they best describe the intellectual dimension.
3. False - Being resilient, resolving conflict respectfully and managing stress may be affected by the spiritual dimension of wellness, but they best describe the emotional dimension of wellness.
4. False - The likelihood of a person developing a wellness lifestyle is influenced by personal choice and their social environment.
5. True.
6. False - Research suggests that high levels of perceived personal energy may help to protect against distress and even contribute to overall happiness.
7. True.
8. False - A person who has short bursts of high energy is a sprinter.
9. False - The two key dimensions of energy are endurance and intensity.
10. True.

CHAPTER 4

1. True.
2. False - The autonomic nervous system (ANS) is divided into the sympathetic and the parasympathetic nervous systems. The CNS (central nervous system) is made up of the brain and the spinal cord.
3. False - The pituitary gland is the "master" gland of the endocrine (hormonal) system. The hypothalamus is considered the key link in the stress response because it controls the sympathetic and parasympathetic nervous systems and the endocrine system.
4. False - Epinephrine and adrenaline are the same hormone. The two main catecholamines that are responsible for providing energy during the stress response are adrenaline and noradrenaline or epinephrine and norepinephrine.
5. True.
6. False - The adrenal medulla secretes the catecholamines into the bloodstream when it is stimulated by the sympathetic nervous system. The adrenal cortex is stimulated by the pituitary gland by the secretion of ACTH (adrenocorticotropic hormone).
7. True.
8. True.
9. False - Your body mobilizes additional resources to re-establish homeostasis during the resistance stage. During the alarm stage, your body is preparing for fight-or-flight.
10. True.

CHAPTER 5

1. True.
2. False - Quantitative overload results from too much to do in the time available. Qualitative overload results from impossibly demanding expectations (no matter how much time you had, you wouldn't be able to perform the task expected because you lack the skills, knowledge or resources).
3. False - Anticipatory stress can result in either distress or eustress, depending on a person's interpretation and ability to cope.
4. True.
5. True.
6. False - The three zones that each person possesses include: a zone of positive stress, a zone of overload stress, and a zone of underload stress.
7. True.
8. False - Stress-seekers thrive on challenge, risk, and sensation.
9. False - A distress-reducer is a person who seeks to do everything possible to promote the well-being of others and to minimize distress for them.
10. True.

CHAPTER 6

1. False - All emotional distress symptoms are multi-faceted. They affect not only one's emotional well-being, but one's behavioral, cognitive, and physical well-being as well.
2. False - Depression is often referred to as the "common cold" of emotional disorders.
3. True.
4. True.
5. False - Thoughts such as "should have," "could have," and "would have" tend to cause guilt.
6. False - When people feel guilty they usually try to make amends because they have done something wrong, but when people feel shame they often isolate themselves from others.
7. False - A nervous breakdown has nothing to do with a breakdown of nerves or the nervous system. Usually it refers to a feeling of helplessness, loss of control, or confusion in a temporary crisis.
8. False - Fuzzy thinking, forgetfulness, and nightmares are all examples of cognitive distress symptoms.
9. False - Irritability, withdrawal, and being easily startled are direct behavioral distress symptoms because they directly reflect internal tension.
10. False - Because all of the distress symptoms are multi-faceted, they most often occur together. For example, when one suffers from depression, emotional distress symptoms (sadness), behavioral distress symptoms (irritability), cognitive distress symptoms (inability to concentrate) and physical distress symptoms (insomnia) can all be experienced at the same time.

CHAPTER 7

1. False - The supply-side approach to health care reform emphasizes treatment. The demand-side approach focuses on prevention.
2. True.
3. False - A blood pressure reading of 140/90 is referred to as borderline hypertension. A blood pressure reading of 120/70 would be considered normal blood pressure.
4. False - Diastolic blood pressure refers to the amount of pressure on the inside walls of blood vessels at the moment of relaxation between heart beats. Systolic blood pressure refers to the amount of pressure on the inside walls of blood vessels at the moment of contraction.
5. False - LDLs (low density lipoproteins) are considered the "bad guys" because they contribute to plaque buildup. HDLs (high density lipoproteins) are considered the "good guys" because they discard cholesterol to the liver.
6. True.
7. False - Rheumatoid arthritis is an autoimmune disease.
8. True.
9. False - Stress plays more of a role in the development of duodenal ulcers. Peptic ulcers are caused by a bacterium.
10. False - Onset insomnia is the type of insomnia when a person can't fall asleep. Chronic insomnia refers to insomnia that is ongoing.

CHAPTER 8

1. False - The two major influences that shape one's personality are environmental influences (nurture factors) and genetics (innate factors). Family and friends are both examples of environmental influences.
2. False - The A in Type A could stand for a lot of "A" words, but it doesn't represent any particular characteristic. Friedman and Rosenman, the researchers who coined the term Type A, meant the name to be very general so as not to offend the psychiatrists who reviewed grant applications.
3. False - As early as the seventeenth century, some physicians spoke of the link between emotions and heart problems.
4. False - Hostility is the most toxic element of Type A behavior.
5. True.
6. True.
7. True.
8. False - A number of studies strongly suggest that Type A behavior can be changed.
9. False - Type A behavior can remain latent or can be exaggerated, depending on the social situation.
10. True.

Harcourt, Inc.

CHAPTER 9

1. False - The two types of perfectionists described in Chapter 9 are internal and external perfectionists.
2. False - Research has shown that perfectionism can severely block one's productivity and creativity.
3. False - Being preoccupied with "shoulds," engaging in all-or-nothing thinking, and overgeneralizing are common characteristics of a perfectionist.
4. True.
5. True.
6. True.
7. False - Learned pessimism includes the tendency to interpret bad events as internally caused, permanent, and universal. A learned pessimist interprets good events as being externally caused, temporary, and specific.
8. True.
9. False - Caretaking, low self-esteem, weak boundaries, and controlling are all characteristics of the codependent personality pattern.
10. True.

CHAPTER 10

1. False - The main difference between Type A's and Type B's is that Type B's possess adequate self-esteem and Type A's do not.
2. False - The belief that Type B's are usually unmotivated to succeed and do not work very hard is a false one. Type B's can be every bit as motivated and productive, if not more so, as Type A's.
3. True.
4. False - Learned optimism involves interpreting good events as being internally caused, permanent, and universal. Learned optimists interpret bad events as being externally caused, temporary, and specific.
5. False - The three C's of hardiness are challenge, commitment, and control. Challenge, confidence, and control are the three C's of the Type C pattern.
6. True.
7. False - The sense of coherence theory refers to the belief that one's life makes sense, one has the resources to cope with daily demands and that those demands are worth expending energy.
8. False - The trait most often found in survivors is humor.
9. False - Serendipity refers to someone having a natural tendency to respond with insight and wisdom under the pressure of an accident or other misfortune. Synergy refers to people who naturally make things go well for themselves and others.
10. True.

Harcourt, Inc.

CHAPTER 11

1. False - Sociological imagination refers to the understanding that personal experiences are influenced by larger social forces.
2. True.
3. False - Social change refers to change in the world outside the person (e.g., population growth, change in the stock market, and technological growth). Personal change refers to changes in the individual's life (e.g., moving, changing job, and starting a regular exercise program).
4. False - Seligman suggests the rate of depression has risen roughly ten-fold over the last two generations.
5. True.
6. False - The three types of transitions that stand out as especially significant for many people are geographic mobility, role transition, and lifestyle change.
7. True.
8. False - It seems to be the accumulation of daily hassles rather than large negative events that wears the individual down mentally and physically.
9. False - Normlessness is the form of alienation that explains the belief that socially unapproved behaviors are necessary and justified to achieve one's goal. Self-estrangement is the sense of being separated from the fruits of one's labor.
10. True.

CHAPTER 12

1. False - Coping is an ongoing, dynamic, and interactional process.
2. True.
3. False - When you assess your resources for dealing with a stressor, you are engaged in secondary appraisal. Primary appraisal of the stressor includes deciding whether or not the stressor is worth being concerned about.
4. True.
5. False - If you react with little awareness or deliberate choice, you are using a scripted coping response. If you respond with thoughtfulness and intention, you are using a deliberate coping response. Both of these responses can be either negative or positive.
6. True.
7. False - Organizing time more effectively during final exam week is an example of problem-focused coping because you are attempting to deal constructively with the stressor. Emotion-focused coping involves dealing with your own fear, anger, guilt, or other emotion as you react to the stressor.
8. False - Hardiness is likely to lead to transformational coping. Regressive coping is thinking pessimistically and avoiding the stressor.
9. True.
10. True.

Harcourt, Inc.

CHAPTER 13

1. True.
2. True.
3. False - Sympathomimetic agents, such as coffee, cola, tea, and chocolate, stimulate the stress response through activation of the sympathetic system. Not only do they increase baseline arousal level, they also increase reactivity.
4. False - According to the Food Guide Pyramid, a person should consume six to eleven servings of the bread, cereal, rice, and pasta group.
5. False - HDL (high density lipoprotein) is the "good guy" of cholesterol because it actually takes the cholesterol to the liver where it is broken down. LDL (low density lipoprotein) is the "bad guy" of cholesterol because it aids in atherosclerosis (plaque formation in the coronary arteries).
6. False - In general, eating a balanced diet rich in fruits and vegetables will yield sufficient vitamins and minerals to meet daily needs.
7. True.
8. False - Studies have shown that eating small meals throughout the day combined with several snacks is better than eating three big meals a day.
9. False - The deepest sleep a person experiences occurs during stage four of NREM. A person's most vivid and intense dreaming occurs during REM sleep.
10. True.

CHAPTER 14

1. True.
2. True.
3. False - The self-talk statement "I know he is upset because of what I said to him earlier" is an example of personalizing. "There are nothing but problems in this relationship" is an example of negativizing.
4. False - In the P & Q method, the P stands for pause and the Q stands for question.
5. False - The three C's of Instant Replay used for managing situational self-talk are catch it, challenge it, and change it.
6. False - Disputation involves challenging and changing one's irrational beliefs.
7. False - The vicious cycle is caused by a negative belief.
8. False - For new self-talk messages to be effective, they should be in the present-tense.
9. True.
10. False - Anger can be positive when it leads to constructive coping.

Harcourt, Inc.

CHAPTER 15

1. False - The relaxation response is controlled through the parasympathetic nervous system and the endocrine system.
2. False - Aerobic exercise is a hypermetabolic approach to stress control. Deep relaxation is a hypometabolic approach to stress control.
3. True.
4. False - Contemplation refers to thinking about the meaning of something. Meditation is first and foremost a method of quieting by using a repeated internal focus to turn down normal thought processes. It does not involve thinking.
5. False - Zen meditation calls for focusing on breathing. Open meditation differs from the other techniques in that one allows the mind to wander and drift.
6. True.
7. True.
8. True.
9. False - Autogenics is practiced by focusing self-suggestions of warmth and heaviness in specific muscle groups throughout the body. Progressive muscle relaxation involves alternately tensing and relaxing specific muscles throughout the body for ten seconds or so. It involves switching between eliciting the sympathetic and the parasympathetic nervous systems--the emergency and calming branches of the autonomic nervous system.
10. True.

CHAPTER 16

1. True.
2. True.
3. False - The experience of social roles, obligations, and commitments that are easy to get into and difficult to get out of is called lifestyle trap.
4. False - The three categories of time-management principles and techniques are prioritizing, scheduling, and implementing.
5. False - The ABC technique is a method of prioritizing tasks.
6. False - Time mapping involves breaking each hour down into detailed segments and assigning a task to each segment. Time blocking involves blocking out several hours on a given day for a specific activity.
7. True.
8. True.
9. False - Chronic time urgency is the combined result of external pressures and our internal beliefs about time.
10. True.

CHAPTER 17

1. False - Social support refers to relationships that bring positive benefits to the individual. Social network refers to the specific set of linkages among a defined set of persons or a given person.
2. False - The most important way true social support takes place in groups is through the informal, incidental contacts that occur outside the central activity.
3. False - When Sam's family and friends provided significant support for him when he lost his wife of 25 years and, as a result, he did not get sick once, this illustrated the buffering effect of social support.
4. True.
5. True.
6. False - A person who too quickly and too completely reveals himself is known as a plunger.
7. True.
8. True.
9. False - Assertiveness is desirable behavior for reducing tension in situations where there is potential buildup of resentment or anger.
10. True.

CHAPTER 18

1. True.
2. False - Constructive maladjustment refers to people who are appropriately concerned about social conditions and they are motivated to change those conditions.
3. False - Self-transcendence refers to taking a person outside himself or herself.
4. True.
5. True.
6. True.
7. False - Helping strangers has been found to be more strongly associated with good health than helping family and friends.
8. True.
9. False - A person experiences both social and personal barriers in the assumption of social responsibility.
10. False - Cultural lag refers to the difficulty in adapting our way of life to technological change.

Harcourt, Inc.

REFERENCES

Butler, P. E. (1981). *Talking to yourself: Learning the language of self-support.* New York: Harper & Row.

Cook, W. & Medley, D. (1954). Proposed hostility and pharasaic-virtue scales for the MMPI. *Journal of Applied Psychology, 38*, 414-18.

Davis, F. (1980). *Personal peak performance: Making the most of your natural energy.* New York: McGraw-Hill.

Gallup Poll. (1994). Between city survey on hostility.

Holmes, T. H. & Rahe, R. H. (1967). The social readjustment rating scale. *Journal of Psychosomatic Research*, 11, 213.

Schlossberg, N. K. (1989). *Overwhelmed: Coping with life's ups and downs.* Lexington, MA: Lexington Books.

Walter, T., & Siebert, A. (1999). *Student success* (8th ed.). Fort Worth: Holt, Rinehart & Winston.

Harcourt, Inc.